Routledge Revivals

DICTIONARY OF THE ORGAN

DICTIONARY OF THE ORGAN

ORGAN REGISTERS, THEIR TIMBRES, COMBINATIONS, AND ACOUSTIC PHENOMENA

BY

CARL LOCHER

ORGELINSPEKTOR DER STADT BERN

AUTHORISED TRANSLATION FROM THE FOURTH (1912) GERMAN EDITION

BY

CLAUDE P. LANDI, L.R.A.M.

First published in 1914 by Kegan Paul, Trench, Trubner & Co., Ltd

This edition first published in 2018 by Routledge
2 Park Square, Milton Park, Abingdon, Oxon, OX14 4RN
and by Routledge
711 Third Avenue, New York, NY 10017

Routledge is an imprint of the Taylor & Francis Group, an informa business

©1914 Taylor & francis.

All rights reserved. No part of this book may be reprinted or reproduced or utilised in any form or by any electronic, mechanical, or other means, now known or hereafter invented, including photocopying and recording, or in any information storage or retrieval system, without permission in writing from the publishers.

Publisher's Note

The publisher has gone to great lengths to ensure the quality of this reprint but points out that some imperfections in the original copies may be apparent.

Disclaimer

The publisher has made every effort to trace copyright holders and welcomes correspondence from those they have been unable to contact.

A Library of Congress record exists under ISBN: 84132616

ISBN 13: 978-1-138-55090-2 (hbk)
ISBN 13: 978-1-138-56592-0 (pbk)
ISBN 13: 978-1-315-12321-9 (ebk)

DICTIONARY OF THE ORGAN

AUTHORISED EDITIONS OF THE PRESENT WORK

German Edition :		*Emil Baumgart*, Bern.
French	do.	*Fischbacher*, Paris.
English	do.	*Kegan Paul, Trench, Trübner, & Co., Ltd.* London.
Italian	do.	*Ulrico Hoepli*, Milano.
"Braille"	do.	*Blinden-Lehrmittel-Verlag*, Illzach.
Finnish	do.	*Paivalehden Kirjapainossa*, Helsingfors.
Dutch	do.	*J. De Zeuw*, Dortrecht.
Spanish	do.	*Gustavo Gili*, Barcelona.
Swedish	do.	*P. A. Norstedt & Soener*, Stockholm.
Danish	do.	*Andr. Fred. Höst & Sön*, Kjóbenhavn.
Esperanto	do.	*In preparation.*

All rights of translation reserved.   Reproduction forbidden.
Even the smallest extracts from this work are forbidden without the author's permission.

DICTIONARY OF THE ORGAN

ORGAN REGISTERS, THEIR TIMBRES, COMBINATIONS, AND ACOUSTIC PHENOMENA

BY

CARL LOCHER
ORGELINSPEKTOR DER STADT BERN

AUTHORISED TRANSLATION FROM THE FOURTH (1912) GERMAN EDITION

BY

CLAUDE P. LANDI, L.R.A.M.

LONDON
KEGAN PAUL, TRENCH, TRÜBNER, & CO., LTD.
BROADWAY HOUSE, 68–74 CARTER LANE, E.C.
1914

INSCRIBED

BY THE TRANSLATOR

TO THE

ROYAL COLLEGE OF ORGANISTS

AUTHOR'S PREFACE TO THE SECOND ENGLISH EDITION

THE appearance of this, the second English edition of my book on the Organ-Stops, affords me the opportunity of expressing my warmest thanks to my English and American colleagues for the sympathetic reception given to the first edition.

Many experts in physics and acoustics, as well as organists, organ-builders, and several Colleges of Music, have recognised the pressing need for some such book of reference, and have most kindly welcomed these results of my fifty years' research work as organist and organ expert.

The high repute of the translator and the well-known name of the publishers will suffice to assure the public that in this new English edition all the latest demands of organ-building, as well as the many recent improvements, have duly been taken into consideration.

I therefore venture to offer this book to all those interested in that king of instruments, the organ; for those who are interested know that in the organ we have the most valuable instrument for the comforting and uplifting of the human soul.

CARL LOCHER.

AUTHOR'S PREFACE TO THE FOURTH GERMAN EDITION

My revision of this modest treatise, undertaken with the greatest conscientiousness and after repeated new journeys, comes in the fiftieth year of my organistic activities. The aids to playing have been in latter years partly increased, partly considerably improved; and the art of voicing has been greatly developed. I may mention, for instance, the many super- and sub-octave couplers; the melodic coupler; the effective Echo and Swell contrivances of every kind; the interesting suggestions of Silbermann; the new simplification in the electric blowing apparatus; the practically regulated register-transmission; the impressive voicing of certain flue stops by means of partly reduced air-pressure; the increasing brilliancy and endurance of the reed stops; the convenient disposition of the draw-knobs.

It was therefore made easier for me to complete in a thorough manner the combination of the various registers by means of carefully carried-out experiments on the new organs of various countries, and thus make varied registration possible even on the smallest instrument. Also, those portions of the

PREFACE TO THE FOURTH GERMAN EDITION

book more closely related to tone-sensations have been amplified and brought thoroughly up to date. In spite of this, however, much of note has no doubt escaped my notice.

I have, as formerly, tried to compress the wealth of material into the smallest possible compass, in order not to exceed to any great extent the former bulk of the book. This circumstance must be my excuse for the use of abbreviations and lack of elegance, which could not well be avoided.

I am very glad to take here the opportunity of expressing my thanks to my learned colleagues—fellow-organists, experts, and organ-builders—who were kind enough to support me with repeated encouragement and useful suggestions, thus making possible this work, which has now spread over into so many countries. I may say that suggestions and information of any kind will at all times be welcomed by me.

The co-operation of my dear friend and colleague, Herr Musik-Direktor J. Luz, organist at the Fraumünster in Zürich, was of especial value to me in amplifying and critically revising this new edition.

C. L.

TRANSLATOR'S NOTE

SINCE the publication of the first English edition of Herr Locher's book in 1888, a number of excellent works on organ-construction have appeared in England. The present translation has been made from the fourth German edition (1912). No apology should be needed for presenting to English readers a new and up-to-date edition of a work which has been translated into *eight* different languages (as well as a "Braille" edition) in addition to the English language, and which has met with universal and unqualified approval among musicians and scientists, chief among whom should be cited the great Helmholtz, to whom Herr Locher dedicated the original edition. The book contains a vast amount of information which is not to be found elsewhere. Herr Locher's knowledge of Continental organs is unequalled, and this should offset the somewhat scanty reference to the magnificent work of English builders, due solely to the fact that Herr Locher is not well acquainted with this country. I am therefore responsible for a separate chapter, in which I have endeavoured to sketch the progress of organ-building in this country. I am indebted to the Rev. J. H. Burn, of Ballater, for drawing my attention to several slight inaccuracies, and for some interesting references to notable instruments built since the appearance of the last German edition of Herr Locher's book—such as the 187-stop organ in the Centennial Hall, Breslau, and the Liverpool Cathedral organ.

C. P. L.

DICTIONARY OF THE ORGAN

A

Accentcoppel. See ELECTRO-PNEUMATIC.

Acoustic Phenomena. See SUBBASS.

Acoustic Tones. See QUINT.

Acuta. See SHARP and MIXTURE.

Æoline derives its name from the Æolian Harp. (A charming description of this ancient instrument is to be found in Radau's *Theory of Sound*.) It is of soft, string-toned character, and is found in nearly all large as well as small new organs as an 8′ solo stop. It is regarded as the softest of string-toned stops. It is met with in the Passau Cathedral organ as Æolian Harp 4′. The pipes of the Æoline are properly of tin; but as the art of organ-building to-day is capable of making the transition from wood to metal imperceptible, the lower notes of this and of some other stops may be constructed of wood, especially where cost is a consideration, provided

1

this is expressly stipulated for in the contract. Arbitrary changes in the materials should not, however, be tolerated. This stop is also met with, at times, as an 8' or 16' reed (see Töpfer, *Orgelbaukunst*, vol. i., § 180), either like the Physharmonica or surmounted by a small bell. I found in the large Cathedral organ at Riga (Walcker) an Ælodicon 16', closely related to the Æoline, as a reed stop on the 2nd manual, and the above-described Æoline as a flue stop on the 4th manual. This stop is now found so frequently in this character, that it would be superfluous to cite further instances of its appearance. I found a 16' Æoline as a reed stop on the 3rd manual of the new organ at The Hague. The Æoline blends well with the Voix céleste (*q.v.*), which is tuned slightly sharper; also with the Wienerflöte and Lieblich-Gedackt. One can advantageously add to this combination the more incisive character of a Flauto Traverso or of a Flûte d'Amour, especially if the Lieblich-Gedackt used is a 16' one and if the stops are enclosed in a swell-box (see CRESCENDO). The 16' Subbass may be made more definite by means of a coupled Æoline, Salicional, Dolce, etc. (see respective articles). The new and increased coupling facilities (super-octave and sub-octave couplers) make possible some charming effects; for instance, by a judicious use of the indispensable swell pedal, the swelling and diminishing sounds of the Æoline with couplers may be artistically accompanied on another manual by a soft Lieblich-Gedackt. An occasional and judicious use of the tremolo with the Lieblich-Gedackt will be found effective; and in certain passages the combination of the Voix céleste with closed swell secures an effect which may be poetically compared to the falling of gentle rain in spring. Should the sub-octave coupler be dispensed with, a soft Lieblich-Gedackt 16' or Salicional 16', combined again with another kind of Æoline (Dolce, etc.) or Voix céleste, provides an interesting and solemn foundation in another way (see VOIX CÉLESTE). Even in the case of the smallest organs the justified demand for one, and in larger organs for two or three, swell-boxes, is universally recognized, their usefulness and effectiveness having been abundantly demonstrated. By means of the super- and sub-octave couplers and of the combination of Æoline and Voix céleste, a kind of Physharmonica effect is obtained in the swelling and diminishing of certain chords, especially in the lower notes. This can be easily tested.

For Clavæoline and physical generation of tone in flue pipes, see respective articles.

The extreme delicacy of the Æoline renders it peculiarly apt for exercising the ear in distinguishing the "nuances" of the various timbres. I would strongly urge the beginner to study carefully the effect of the Æoline or of the Salicional combined with a flute stop of precise intonation, such as an 8' flute or a Flauto Traverso. Let him also compare, from the point of view of the intensity of sound, the Æoline with the Gamba or the Viola, the Salicional or the Dolce—all stops of the same family.

The employment of the "crescendo" will demonstrate yet more clearly and strikingly to an untrained ear the "nuances" of the timbre of these Gamba stops. It will be at the same time excellent practice in learning how to use the swell. (See also REGISTRATION, TIMBRE, and CRESCENDO.)

Æolian Bass. The Bros. Jehmlich, of Dresden, have had the happy idea of placing in the Kreuzkirche in Dresden, in addition to a Dulcian Bass 16′, an Æolian Bass 16′, as a pedal stop.

Æolian Harp. See ÆOLINE.

Aliquot. See QUINT.

Amorosa. See FLÛTE D'AMOUR.

Ausschaltungen (annulling pistons). See TRUMPET.

Auswechslung. "Exchange." A contrivance which annuls the stops of a given manual and brings into play those of the Echo organ (*e.g.* Enge, Zürich). In the organ in Christ Church, Berne, this result is obtained by drawing the Vox Humana.

Auszug. "Extracts" from mixture stops. In organs which do not possess independent 2′ stops, it should be made possible to borrow, by means of a special button, the 2′ of the Mixture, of the Harmonia Ætherea or other mixture stop, and to use the same separately.

B

Baarpijp (*Dutch*). A clear, 8′ flute stop with metal pipes which I have met with in several organs in the Netherlands.

Baritone. See TUBA MIRABILIS.

Bass Flute. See FLUTE (end of article).

Bass Tuba. See TUBA MIRABILIS.

Bassethorn. A free reed stop, mostly 8′, of Clarinet quality, but softer. It possesses a somewhat melancholy timbre of its own, and I can but recommend its more frequent inclusion in large organs. Walcker has placed a very effective Bassethorn 8′ in the pedal of the Wilhelmkirche organ at Strassburg.

Bassoon (*Ger.*, Fagott). This stop is met with mostly in French organs as a beating reed (with so-called "anches à larmes"). It occurs both as a 16′

and 8′ stop. In its lower notes it imitates fairly well its orchestral prototype. In German and Swiss organs the Bassoon appears generally as a free reed, for the most part 16′, of Clarinet quality. It is found as Fagott 16′ in the Apostelkirche at Cologne (Goll); as Bassoon in the Stadtkirche at Glarus; also on the 3rd manual (swell) of the organ in the new Lutherkirche in Wiesbaden (Walcker), where it appears in company with a Harmonic Trumpet, an Oboe, and a Clarion. (See also PHYSHARMONICA, OBOE, and CLARINET.)

Availing himself of the resources of electricity, the late genial Fr. Columban, Abbot of Einsiedeln, has constructed in one of the Convent churches a Bassoon-Oboe which can be put to various uses: according as to whether one draws out or pushes in the draw-knob, it acts as an 8′ or 16′ manual stop, or as an 8′ pedal stop. (See TRANSMISSION.)

Cantor Gerecke mentions in the *Z. f. I.* (*Zeitschrift für Instrumentenbau*) a contrivance which makes it possible to convert an 8′ stop into a 4′ or 16′, at will. (For electricity applied to organ-building, see ELECTRO-PNEUMATIC). Fine 16′ and 8′ Bassoons have also been placed by Cavaillé-Coll (now Mutin) in the Trocadero organ in Paris.

Bassoon-Oboe. See BASSOON.

Bauernflöte (*Ger.*, "peasant flute"). A 2′ stop placed in the organ in St Michael's, Hamburg.

Bell Gamba (*Ger.*, Glockengambe). The name of a stop found in England, the pipes of which are provided with a kind of cone in the shape of an inverted funnel.

Bifara, tibia bifaris. See DOPPELFLÖTE.

Bombarde. A beating pedal reed, 16′ or 32′, more powerful than the Bassoon, but less so than the Trombone (*q.v.*). In nearly every country, organs are now found in which the 3rd or 4th manual is a so-called Bombarde manual based on the 16′ tone (see Töpfer, part i., § 1265). It becomes more and more evident that swell-boxes are of value only when they contain something really adequate to intensify and decrease, viz., when effects which influence intensively the whole organ can be obtained by their employment.

By means of the new transmission and multiplying contrivances (see TRANSMISSION), it is to-day possible to make the strong reed stops (formerly met with only in the largest instruments) valuable dynamic allies of the swell-box.

For these and many other new developments of the art of organ-building mentioned in this book, I take the opportunity of warmly thanking the various and deserving inventors. For an account of the manner in which sound is produced in reed pipes, see REED STOPS (also CRESCENDO).

Bombardon. See BOMBARDE.

Bordun. See BOURDON.

Bourdon. A covered wood stop, to be found even on the oldest organs, and which, by its massive, full sound, is able to lend to the manual extreme dignity and an ecclesiastical solemnity of tone. The usefulness of this stop also as a solo of 8′ tone, particularly in the upper notes, if well voiced, has latterly been more and more fully recognised. (See also ROHRFLÖTE.) In French organs, the generic name of Bourdon is applied to all covered stops. A 16′ Bourdon on the manuals, if neither size nor material have been spared, gives depth and fulness even to the smallest organ.

For the advantage of a correspondingly narrower Bourdon on the upper manuals as Lieblich- or Still-Gedackt 16′, see also GEDACKT.

A Bourdon or Lieblich-Gedackt 16′ (see also ECHOBASS), is now found even in small organs, either as an independent stop or by means of " borrowing," often on the swell, in order to enable the player to accompany even the softest passages with an adequate pedal bass. (See also GEDACKT.)

The Bourdons are divided into Bourdons proper, Gedackts and Lieblich (Still)-Gedackts, according to the decreasing diameter of the pipes.

There are few combinations in which the Bourdon does not find a place. A specially charming effect is obtained by using a Bourdon with a fine Gamba or a soft Trumpet; or, by coupling, with a reed stop on an upper manual, viz., with swell Oboe, Clarinet, or Viola, employing the swell pedal, and the former maintaining an even amount of tone. (See SWELL-BOX, end of article.) It is by virtue of its facility in blending with no matter which other stop, that the Bourdon was generally called in former times, in German, "Coppelflöte" or "Coppel." (See COPULA, and also REGISTRATION.) Grand Bourdon 32′, see QUINT.

In our days, the pipes of Gedackts are built of metal instead of wood, as was formerly more frequently the case, in order to blend them better with the metal mixtures and to better withstand dampness.

In view of the possibility of rendering imperceptible, to-day, the transition from wood to metal, the exclusive employment of either material is no longer necessary even for this stop.

Bourdonbass. See BOURDON.

C

Calcant und Gebläsemotoren. A draw-stop applied to many organs, serving to call the blower's attention to the bellows. I may say here that I have now and then seen people engaged as blowers who, being the reverse of intelligent, had for that reason been chosen for their apparently inferior position. Through their violent pulling, sudden releasing, and generally incompetent treatment of the blowing apparatus, great expense has been incurred by a parish, which would have paid a thoroughly trained, conscientious blower for years. Sometimes the Calcant is pneumatic (air-pressure bell). See *Z. f. I.*, vol. xx., No. 25.

In almost all new organs, motors are now replacing the Calcant bell.

It is a matter for congratulation to find that the use of gas, water, or electric motors for blowing purposes is becoming more and more general. These motors, with ventilators, have been tested with many modern organs and found to work perfectly.

Herr Dr. Alois von Reding has been good enough to contribute specially for this work the following note relative to the installation of motors:—

"An electric motor destined for blowing purposes should be *sufficiently powerful* and *act silently*. These desiderata can be attained when, in making out the specification, a rational rather than a cheap installation shall be kept in view, and the necessary expense shall not be grudged in consulting an expert *before* the order is placed. Thus will disagreements and possible law-suits be avoided: and the estimate will not be exceeded.

"Very often—especially in connection with small organs—motors of insufficient power are chosen, not having sufficiently taken into account the wear and tear which take place through the rubbing of the parts in the transmissions, ventilators, or bellows, as well as escapes of wind.

"If a future enlargement is contemplated, it is preferable to order in the first place a motor of more than sufficient power, because the ultimate change of motor would cost much more.

"The high speed of small electro-motors up to 4 h.p. used in the trades — more than 1000 revolutions per minute—causes drones and whistling noises which disturb soft playing. This nuisance can be remedied by placing the motor in a sound-proof room. If the motor had to be placed in close proximity to the organ, this and analogous remedies, such as the employment of a box padded with rubber and felt, etc., would not be sufficient to deaden effectively disagreeable noises. In such a case, one employs electro-motors at reduced speed (less than 1000 revolutions per minute), whose noise does not obtrude even during the softest passages, as we have found by experience. Such motors are more expensive than the ordinary ones, but the extra cost is largely compensated by less wear and tear and smaller cost of upkeep.

"With regard to motors with alternating currents, one must always stipulate that they shall not give out rumbling sounds.

"In installations with ventilators, the latter are coupled directly to the electro-motors. The number of revolutions per minute should not exceed 1000;

otherwise the noises would become too prominent; for, although these are covered by the full or moderately loud organ, they become disturbingly noticeable when soft playing is in progress.

"Installations with sucking bellows nearly always demand transmissions. The latter should be sustained exclusively by means of straps: cogged wheels would make too much noise. The bellows must not work too rapidly, because the valves would quickly commence to flap.

"The speed of electro-motors can be regulated automatically within very large limits, so that the engine works more or less rapidly in proportion to the amount of air contained in the reservoir: thus escapes of wind are always compensated.

"Regulating can be accomplished in the simplest manner by means of rheostats acting automatically through the mediation of the air reservoir."

Motors are all the more indispensable to the organist in proportion to the difficulty which he encounters in securing a blower and thus practising as much as he pleases. We therefore think that it is greatly to the advantage of parishes and organists to install a good motor—an electric motor by preference.

In the organ which the builder Heferer, of Agram, has built at Neudorf (Hungary), the bellows is provided with glass valves, which is an advantage in places which are damp or exposed to sudden changes of temperature.

We cannot advise too strongly those in charge of churches or concert-halls to have the premises always sprinkled before they are swept, because the dust causes considerable damage to the organ, very often involving repairs to a relatively new instrument. In the case of concert-halls with upholstery, draperies, and curtains, the use of the electric vacuum cleaner is to be strongly recommended, as in this way the dust will not disperse.

When an organ is erected, one must also protect the bellows—often placed on the floor—from the influences of outside temperature. Effective precautions must also be taken to prevent careless persons from injuring the instrument. I would further recommend the prompt and effective treatment of the case and wooden pipes with "formalin," whenever the slightest signs of wood-worm are observed. Here also serious and far-reaching injury may be prevented. It is an equally good precaution to insure the organ against fire; more than one parish has already learned this to its cost. Finally, the organ must be placed in a thoroughly dry spot; or, failing this, radical measures, such as varnishing, tarring, etc., must be taken against all trace of dampness.

Numerous parishes and colleagues have thanked me for these and similar suggestions.

For the good upkeep of the instrument, it should be thoroughly overhauled (pipes cleaned, etc.) about every five years. (See also SPECIFICATION.)

Campanelli. See CARILLON.

Cardboard used as material for the construction of pipes. See REED STOPS.

Carillon (*Fr.*). Bells (*Ger.*, Glockenspiel; *It.*, Campanelli). An arrangement now frequently met with in large organs, and, in Italy, even in small instruments. The carillon most appropriately finds a place in concert organs, where it is often very effective—as, for instance, in the Trocadero organ in Paris. In the Sydney Town Hall organ is to be found a four-rank carillon in the swell-box. In St Michael's, Hamburg, Walcker has placed two carillons with real bells, one low, of thirty-seven notes, and one high, of forty-nine notes. In the same organ is to be found a four-rank carillon, $2\frac{2}{3}'$, $1\frac{1}{3}'$, $1\frac{1}{7}'$, and $1'$ (clochettes). In the Cathedral at Merseburg is a carillon composed of thirty-seven steel bars with a compass c–c^3 (see C. F. Becker). In St Jacob's, Hamburg, I have found, under the name carillon, copper bells, starting from small a; and in the Braunschweig Cathedral (Furtwängler in Hanover) a carillon with real bronze plates tuned from small f, which give a magnificent effect. I have also seen a superb carillon at Utrecht. For further details respecting the carillon, which is most often met with in the Low Countries, consult Radau, *Lehre vom Schall* ("Theory of Sound"), p. 272.

I have often found, in Italian organs, carillons as

organ stops, starting from c. Sauer has placed a 4′ pneumatic carillon in the pedal department of the Kaiser Wilhelm Gedächtniskirche, Berlin, where it is used with fine effect to emphasise a Canto Fermo. I have also found a very effective carillon in the new organ in the Cathedral at Berlin (Sauer), composed of steel bars extending from ab^2 to c^3, and enclosed in the swell-box of the 3rd manual. Prof. Wolfrum has recently had a carillon placed on the Echo manual of the great concert organ at Heidelberg, built by Voigt. This stop is also met with in the Nicolaikirche at Leipzig (Sauer), Pietermaritzburg, Natal (Brindley & Foster), St Michael's, Hamburg (Walcker), and Christ Church, Mannheim (Steinmeyer), and others.

Under the name of "Clochettes" is found sometimes a three- or four-rank mixture which is delightfully effective, for instance, in the Sydney Town Hall organ (Hill), The Hague (Witte), Lausanne Cathedral (Kuhn), Saint-Eustache, Paris, Saint-Bonaventure, Lyon, Northeim, etc. I have also found beautiful carillons in the excellent organs at The Hague, Haarlem, and Trocadero (Paris). It will be seen from these examples—of which many are cited from recently built organs—that the carillon as a stop is finding favour. An organist of refined taste will nevertheless guard against an excessive use of this stop, a failing which I have often noticed, especially in the south.

'Cello. See Violoncello.

Chalumeau. See Musette and Schalmei.

Choralbass. A pedal stop, rarely found under this name. I have found in several organs of the convent at Einsiedeln two stops labelled Choralbass 3′, giving the effect of a three-rank mixture. In the pedal department of the new Lutheran organ at Wiesbaden, Walcker has placed, in addition to a Rohrflöte 4′, a 4′ Choralbass; and in St Michael's, Hamburg, the same builder has placed a 4′ Choralbass (also in the pedal) with double lips and of principal character.

Clairon (Clarion; a small trumpet) or **Clarino**. A reed stop of narrower scale than the trumpet, but of more decisive and clear timbre. It is found generally as a 4′ pedal stop (more rarely as 2′); sometimes also on the great (Gedächtniskirche, Berlin; St John's, Helsingfors), occasionally also on the secondary manuals (Notre-Dame, Paris). For further particulars regarding this decisive stop, see Trumpet (section Clarino).

Clarabella (Claribella, Claribel) 8′ and 4′. From the Latin *clarus*, clear, and *bellus*, beautiful (and the English *bell*?); or possibly also from the Italian. A flue stop of clear, pleasing tone, resembling an 8′ open flute. It is generally constructed of wood, with wide slots. It figures prominently in all large modern organs of English and American make—for instance, Liverpool, Canterbury, Dundee (Walcker), Birmingham, Garden City, U.S.A.; also in the Town Hall at Pietermaritzburg (Natal), where it is found as a 4′ stop under the name of *Clear Flute*.

Clarinet 8′. A solo stop of brilliant effect, imitating the orchestral instrument of the same name—whence the name of Orchestral Clarinet appearing in the Natal organ mentioned in the article Clarabella. It is of large scale, cylindrical in shape, and provided, like the Trumpet, with conical (also cylindrical) bells. With regard to power, it stands midway between the Oboe and a soft Trumpet. It is satisfactory to note that, thanks to new improvements, this stop is increasingly found of beautiful quality and remains longer in tune (Casino, Berne). A 4′ Clarinet is to be found on the pedal of the Dresden Cathedral organ (Silbermann). The Clarinet blends agreeably with an 8′ Bourdon, or, by coupling, with the Concert or Vienna flute or Flauto Traverso 4′, or, again, with the Flûte d'Amour 4′. (See also BASSOON.)

In organs possessing several swell-boxes, an effective combination may be obtained by accompanying a melody on the Clarinet with soft, full chords on the Voix céleste (*q.v.*), Lieblich-Gedackt 16′ and 8′, and Flûte d'Amour 4′, when these latter stops are not voiced too softly. (See also TRUMPET.) The Clarinet also blends naturally with every Bourdon and with the Flauto Traverso; the addition of the Lieblich-Gedackt 16′, Flauto Dolce 8′, and Rohrflöte 4′, used dynamically, yields interesting tone-colours. Magnificent effects are produced by the following combination: Clarinet 8′, Salicional (or Viola) 8′ and 16′, Flauto Traverso 8′, Geigenprincipal 8′, Fugara 4′. To obtain a martial effect in the melody, a full, round 8′ flute is added by means of the melodic coupler (*q.v.*); this, however, like the previous stop, must be capable of regulation by means of the swell.

One should try, for instance, Reger and Wagner transcriptions with this tone-material, and transfer certain passages (on the afore-mentioned foundation) to the 3rd or 4th manual through a nicely swelling solo trumpet, introducing the Rollschweller in a cautious manner. In great crescendo passages, the 32′ Subbass and an Echo mixture may be interpolated at times. (See TRUMPET, end of article.)

I have had the opportunity of examining, in the factory of the builder Roman Fuchs at Villingen (Grand Duchy of Baden), a Clarinet constructed entirely of wood, the reeds being made out of beech-wood. This experiment seems to have proved successful, and might, we believe, become generalised in time. Similar experiments might doubtless be made with the Vox Humana. Prof. Holzhalb, of Zürich, had, by the way, made similar experiments before. See also SONARPFEIFE.

Clarino. See TRUMPET.

Clavæoline. "In 1830, Beyer, of Naumburg, invented a free-reed 8' stop of very delicate intonation, which he named Clavæoline. This stop is made of copper tongues enclosed in ball-shaped bells. The wind being admitted into the bell through a narrow opening causes the little tongue to vibrate" (Couwenberg *The Organ: Ancient and Modern*, p. 53). For a long time the Clavæoline has been confused with the Æoline.

In the newly-built Wenzell organ at Naumburg, Ladegast mentions an 8' Clavæoline as a reed stop, with the interesting note that the organ was built in 1746, and was examined and taken to pieces by J. S. Bach.

Clochette. See CARILLON.

Collective Coupler (*Ger.*, Generalcoppel). An arrangement which operates simultaneously on all the various couplers. It is of great utility in large organs, as it enables one to employ the various manuals with greater independence. The Collective Coupler must not be confused with the Octave Coupler and with the Tertia Manu (*q.v.*).

Collective Pedals. See COMBINATION REGISTERS.

Collective Registers (from the Latin *colligere*, to unite). Pedals, draw-knobs, or buttons which are drawn or pushed, and which enable the organist to make use simultaneously of all the stops belonging to the same manual or to the same family. In the organ of Saint-Eustache in Paris, for instance, there exists a collective register for the "fonds" (foundation stops) and another for the "anches" (reeds). The Philharmonic organ in Berlin is particularly rich in appliances of this kind, as are also many other large concert and church organs. (See also PROLONGEMENT and COMBINATION REGISTERS.)

Collectiv-Schweller. See CRESCENDO.

Combination Registers. These are also pedals, draw-knobs, or buttons which are drawn or pushed. They enable the organist to prepare in advance, in the course of a piece, whatever combination he may require, bringing it into play at the moment it is wanted. There are combination registers which affect only one manual; there are others which affect the whole organ. There are others, simpler ones, which are met with nearly everywhere. These effect a certain number of stereotyped combinations (according to the number of stops contained in the organ), fixed once for all at the time the organ is erected—combinations which yield from pp to the full organ, and, in large organs, affording six gradations of tone, viz. pp, *p*, *mf*, *f*, *ff*, without reeds, and tutti (full organ). These registers must not be confused with those which unite groups of stops belonging to the same family (gambas, flutes, bourdons, principals). The organ in the Albert Hall, London, also possesses a considerable number of combination stops and pedals—thirty-two buttons for the four manuals, and a number of composition pedals. These aids to playing are becoming always more numerous and of ever-increasing importance in all new organs, even small ones (see COUPLERS); and in certain instruments are to be found as many collective couplers, buttons, tilting-tablets and auxiliary registers of all sorts as there are actual sounding stops. (See PROLONGEMENT, and what is said there concerning this multitude of combinations which often serve only to confuse the organist and prevent him from making personal researches.) For free combinations see REGISTRATION (Stop-Combination). I would also mention here the combination stops (Gamba 8′, Viola 4′, etc.) placed by the Bros. Rieger in the Jägendorf organ.

Concert Flute 8′. In the so-called "Tonhalle" (*q.v.*) called Fernflöte. A wood stop. From *c*′ (more rarely from small *c*) it is sometimes harmonic, with pipes of double length, like the Flauto Traverso. It resembles very much the Viennese Flute, but is fuller and clearer than the latter, although, as a rule, of thinner intonation. The name of Concert Flute is sometimes applied to quite ordinary flute stops. This abuse should not be tolerated. The organs at Apolda and Mulhaus possess fine Concert Flutes on the 3rd manual. (See VIENNA FLUTE, and combinations suggested therein.)

Console (*Ger.*, Spieltischanlagen; *Fr.*, Console des claviers). Herr Rupp, the Strassburg organist, has lately contributed a very interesting article on this subject in the *Z. f. I.*, wherein he recommends that the disposition of the manuals should be such as to make it possible for either hand to play on two manuals at the same time, and thus obtain special effects. I have had numerous opportunities, in my capacity as an organ-expert, to come into contact with arrangements of this kind, and can but endorse the recommendation that the distance between each manual should be rendered more and more convenient. Here I would refer to the well-known Vienna Congress and its results. As I have pointed out elsewhere, an account of the Congress would go beyond the limits of my work. Besides, the attentive reader will have come across, in various passages, my suggestions and hints concerning stops. Finally, I would refer the reader to the chapter on the Console in the brochure on the management of the organ by Musikdirektor Johannes Biehle, of Bautzen; also to the most valuable work of Max Richter on modern aids to organ-playing.

Contrabass (Double Bass). As a 32′ stop (see QUINT) it is acoustically combined with Violin 16′, and Gedackt 10⅔′ (sometimes only 5⅓′ in length, but producing 10⅔′ tone; see GEDACKT). As an open 32′ and 16′ pipe it is always voiced—both as to quality and power—between the Violin Bass and Principal Bass (Open Diapason Bass), which latter stop, especially on French and Belgian organs (*i.e.* those of Annessens and Schyven) it is often called upon to replace.

Organ-builders seem to have always taken especial care in the manufacture of this stop; and its intonation has not varied much since its inception.

In those instruments wherein the Harmonicabass replaces the Violin Bass, the character of a Double Bass is very appropriately imparted to the Principal Bass. (See also SUBBASS and UNTERSATZ.) The builders Steinmeyer at Öttingen and Sauer at Frankfurt on the Oder have placed Contraviolons 32′ in the organs at Rothenburg on the Tauber, in the Frauenkirche at Munich, and in the Willibrordikirche at Wesel. The Contrabass and Contraviolon are very similar, the difference between them, even to a trained ear, being discernible only in the greater prominence of certain harmonics in the latter stop.

Contragamba. See GAMBA.

Contra-Harmonicabass. See HARMONICABASS.

Contraposaune. See TROMBONE.

Contraviolon. See CONTRABASS.

Coppelflöte. See COUPLER.

Copplung (Coppel). See COUPLER.

Cor anglais (*in German*, Englisch Horn). A solo stop of great beauty, whose timbre resembles that of the Horn, and which stands, as regards strength, midway between the Trumpet and the Oboe. It is generally constructed with beating reeds. Nowadays it is frequently met with. The late Prof. Dr Reimann, of Berlin—to whom I am indebted for many valuable suggestions—calls attention to a remarkable Cor anglais 8′, the work of Sauer, in the organ of the German cemetery in Rome. This stop is well represented in Switzerland in the Basle and Lucerne Cathedrals; in the Kaiser Wilhelm Gedächtniskirche, Berlin; also in two small organs at Wohlen (Berne), Bollingen, etc.; also in the Liederhalle at Stuttgart (Weigle), where the stop is on a greater pressure (see TUBA MIRABILIS). It is also found in Saint-Eustache, Paris, and in the Greek Syllogue Concert Hall at Constantinople (Cavaillé-Coll). Finally, this stop is found as a 4′ stop in the Stadthalle of Heidelberg (Voit) and in St Michael's, Hamburg (Walcker). In the case of small organs, containing only one or two reed stops, I should like to see in the swell a Gieseke Clarinet (*q.v.*), which keeps well in tune, and for the simple reason that the tone of the Cor anglais in some respects resembles that of a Trumpet, whereas a well-voiced orchestral-like Clarinet is of an entirely different character.

Cor de nuit. See NACHTHORN.

Cormorne (also called Cromorne, Cremorne, Krummhorn; *lit.*, a crooked horn). An 8′ reed stop of soft intonation, resembling the Horn (Notre-Dame and Trocadero, Paris; Birmingham). I have found at Antwerp a Cormorne of characteristic effect (see also OPHICLEIDE), and, with the designation Krumhoorn 8′, the same stop in St Lawrence's, Rotterdam. In English organs the Cormorne is sometimes voiced like a Clarinet. See also the article COR DE NUIT, which resembles the Cormorne.

J. Dobler has placed in the Seminarkirche in Zug a Krummhorn (beating) which may be used in many different ways, of beautiful trumpet-like tone, between an English Horn and a Trumpet, but of a little darker timbre than the latter.

Cornet à piston. A manual stop resembling its orchestral prototype. It appears as an 8′ stop in the organ at Pietermaritzburg (Natal).

Cornet harmonique. See CORNET.

Cornett (or Cornet). A kind of mixture stop. It is based upon the natural scale, and is made up of the tonic 8′, octave 4′, quint $2\frac{2}{3}$′, fifteenth 2′, and tierce $1\frac{3}{5}$′. The three- and four-rank Cornets do not yield the higher harmonics. Sometimes the Cornet is based upon the 16′ tone. Such is the case in St John's, Schaffhausen; Lausanne Cathedral (Kuhn); Boston (U.S.A.) Music Hall. A four-rank Cornettbass 16′ is found in St Elisabeth's, Breslau (Schlag).

In St. Michael's, Hamburg, Walcker has placed a very effective four-rank Cornet 16′ with quint $2\frac{2}{3}$′ and tierce $1\frac{3}{5}$′—employing a quint $5\frac{1}{3}$′ and violin 4′ as a pedal stop enclosed in the fourth manual swell-box.

Goll, of Lucerne, has placed a beautiful three-rank Cornet, acting as an Echo mixture, on the fourth manual of the Berne Cathedral organ, rebuilt by him. This stop is not satisfactory unless all the notes or tones of its composition blend so homogeneously that no particular one among them predominates (see Töpfer, *Lehrbuch der Orgelbaukunst* ("Treatise on Organ-building"), pt. i. p. 97). The scale of the Cornet is comparatively the widest employed in the construction of organ pipes, and is the only mixture stop which does not "break"; whereas other mixture stops often "break" in the upper octaves (see MIXTURES). A well-made Cornet lends much volume to the organ; its intonation is loud, and its tone resembles that of the Horn, from which it derives its name (from the Latin *cornu*, a horn).

The Cornet is one of the few mixture stops which can be employed as a brilliant solo, naturally only in combination with foundation flue stops of equal scale. In the Pilsen organ, for instance, there is a three-rank Cornet $5\frac{1}{3}'$ (*g c e*) labelled Solo Cornet. In the Cathedral at Schwerin is found—a rare thing—a Cornet *g c e b*. For small organs, the organist Dobler recommends the following composition for the Cornet: C 8', *g* $2\frac{2}{3}'$, *c* 2', *e* $1\frac{3}{5}'$, and *c* 1'.

Cornettin. A five-rank mixture stop, *g b c d e*, with the 3rd and 7th tempered, which, according to Schneider and Frenzel, is advisable in this composition. It is found in the Schneeberg organ (Saxony).

Cornettino $2\frac{2}{3}'$ (as a three-rank stop, narrow scale, $2\frac{2}{3}'$, 2', and $1\frac{3}{5}'$). A mixture stop which Goll has placed with excellent results in the upper manuals of many organs, to replace the Mixture proper.

Corno. See CORNOPEAN.

Cornopean (from the Latin *cornu*, a horn, and the English "pæan," a song of praise). An 8' stop resembling the Horn. It is often met with in modern English and American organs, mostly placed in the swell, together with the Oboe. Walcker, in the new

Votivkirche organ in Vienna, has placed a Corno 4 among the beating reeds. William Hill has placed a Cornopean 8′ in the organ in Westminster Abbey, London, as well as in the Sydney Town Hall organ. Brindley & Foster have also placed it in the Pietermaritzburg (Natal) organ, together with a Horn and an Oboe. (Of course the Cornopean is quite common in English organs.—TR.)

Coupler (*Ger.*, Coppel or Copplung). By Coupler is intended a mechanism which permits the stops of several manuals to be played upon one.

The Great to Pedal coupler is found in all organs; but it is advantageous to be able to couple also other manuals to the pedal, such an arrangement enabling a skilful player, when accompanying a soft solo stop, to define or reinforce discreetly the Subbass, Harmonicabass or Echo Bass with a soft stop belonging to one of the other manuals. It is with this object in view that certain organs possess a mechanism which permits the use of the Lieblich-Gedackt 16′ as an Echo Bass on the Pedal. (See also TRANSMISSION.)

For the octave coupler in the Convent at Einsiedeln, acting on the upper manuals, see OCTAVE COUPLER. I cannot too strongly urge the necessity of studying thoroughly the combinations which the various couplers offer. The variety of tone-colours which may often be produced by simply coupling the stops of different manuals—even in organs containing a very limited number of stops—is surprising. (See ÆOLINE.)

The judicious employment of the sub- and super-octave couplers from one manual to another and upon the same manual (see ÆOLINE and OCTAVE COUPLER) affords an able organist a splendid source from which to draw some beautiful effects. To this are added the tone-colours to be obtained from the use of the swell, Rollschweller, etc., which are becoming increasingly indispensable. (See end of article on DOPPELFLÖTE, also especially OCTAVE COUPLER.)

I would recommend to parishes ordering new organs not to grudge couplers, collective registers, free combinations, and, above all, a well-made swell-box. (See also STOP COMBINATIONS, CRESCENDO, and TRANSMISSIONS.)

Coupler is further the obsolete name of a *real stop*, and is used in that sense as a diminutive of the word Coppelflöte, because it may be combined with every other stop. It is usually made with stopped pipes, and is found in a threefold capacity, *i.e.* 16′, 8′, and 4′. The name Coupler for an actual stop, however, is no longer used at the present day, but is substituted by Bourdon or Gedackt (see BOURDON). Cantor Gericke has made suggestions in the *Z. f. I.* with reference to a special octave coupler by means of which every normal stop could be employed in a threefold capacity. (See also OCTAVE COUPLER and TRANSMISSIONS.)

Crescendo. See SWELL-BOX.

Cymbal (*Ger.*, Cymbel; *Fr.*, Cymbale). A mixture stop of narrow scale, which, on account of its small pipes, is the acutest of all the mixtures; it is consequently the last stop to draw for the full organ. The large Sydney Town Hall organ (126 stops) has a four-rank Cymbal; that of Cincinnati a seven-rank Cymbal; that at Wesel has a Gross-Cymbel. A $2\frac{2}{3}'$ Cymbal (three-rank) is found in the Town Hall at Heidelberg (Voit); also a three-rank Cymbel in the Tonhalle (*q.v.*) at Düsseldorf (Sauer). I have also found a powerful three-rank Gross-Cymbel in the new organ in the Cathedral, Berlin (Sauer). With reference to the Cymbal in the twelfth century, *vide* an article by Max Allihn in the *Z. f. I.*, 22nd year.

Cymbelstern. An obsolete stop. *Vide* Pirro, *L'orgue de J. S. Bach*.

D

Deutsche Flöte. See WIENERFLÖTE (Vienna Flute).

Diapason. This name denotes not only a tuning-fork, but, in organ-building, applies also to the stops Principal, Octave, and Gedackt [these three terms being here used in their Continental meaning. What is known in England as a Diapason is called by the Germans *Principal*, and by the French *Montre*. The "Octave" is equivalent to our *Principal*. "Gedackt" (a corruption of Gedeckt) is a generic German term meaning "covered" or "stopped."— Tr.]. It is met with in many French and in all English organs (for instance, Westminster Abbey. London; Town Hall, Sydney; St. Hélier, etc.), where it frequently occurs in all four manuals as Double Diapason 16' or Double Open Diapason 16' (equivalent to Principal 16'), Open Diapason 8', Small Stopped Diapason (Lieblich-Gedackt), Stopped Diapason (Gedackt) 8'; and in the Pedal a Double Open Diapason 32' occurs, which is equivalent to the Principalbass, The 4' Octave, so important for tuning (vide Tempera-ment), is labelled Principal 4'.

Seidel, in his work, adopts the term Disdiapason for the Super-Octave. Roosevelt (New York) adopts in all his organs the name Violin Diapason for the Geigenprincipal 8'.

Differential Tones. See Quint.

Discanttrompete. See Trumpet.

Disposition. See Specification.

Dolce 8'. A stop of the Salicional family, with metal pipes, generally conical, widening at the top, and of somewhat larger scale than the Salicional. It is an exquisite, soft stop which should appear on the Great manual of all large organs, in order that this manual should possess a softer string-toned stop than the naturally more powerful Gamba, Some builders (*i.e.* Weigle) voice this stop soft and flute-like, without the biting quality, like a Flauto Dolce. It is frequently found as Dolcissimo 4'.

Concerning the employment of wood for the lower notes, see ÆOLINE.

The Dolce blends agreeably with the Bourdon 8', Hohlflöte 8', Flauto Traverso 4', or Flûte d'Amour; and, by coupling, with a Vienna Flute 8' or Lieblich-Gedackt 8' and 4', placed in a swell-box. It is equally valuable to define the somewhat vague intonation of the Subbass 16', where a Violoncello would be too powerful. A melody rendered by the Dolce acquires a charming tint when accompanied by the Voix celeste and a Lieblich-Gedackt 16' enclosed in a swell-box. (See also VOICING.)

The Dolce is also useful, when used with the melodic coupler (*q.v.*), to lend a fine precision to the leading voice of an upper manual, *i.e.* Flauto Traverso 8' or Gedackt 8', or Voix céleste (*q.v.*). In order, on the other hand, to brighten in an effective manner by means of the melodic coupler a combination of, for instance, Salicional 16', Salicional or Geigenprincipal 8', and Fugara 4' on an upper manual, the Lieblich-Gedackt 8' or a soft, wide-scale Flute 8' renders admirable service.

Dolciano. A kind of Flute with open pipes, made of wood; rarely found (Görlitz).

Dolcissimo. See DOLCE.

Doppelflöte (Double Flute). A Flute with pipes made of wood, both open and stopped, generally 8′, and provided with two mouths or lips placed opposite to each other, and having, consequently, also two slots. Its tone, therefore, is brighter than that of a single Flute. It is sometimes met with under the name of Duiflöte or Jubalflöte (*q.v.*). The Doppelflöte brightens considerably the Gamba 8′. The second Pedal of the Marienkirche at Lübeck contains a double-lipped Bass Flute 16′ (see HOHLFLÖTE); and a double-lipped Rohrflöte (*q.v.*) occurs in the Breslau Cathedral organ. Walcker has placed in an organ in St Petersburg a two-rank Bifara, the first of which is an 8′ stopped, and the second a 4′ open (Dolce). The Berne Cathedral organ boasts of a fine Doppelflöte; also the organ in St Paul's, Berlin, and that of Temple-du-Bas, Neuchâtel.

A magnificent effect may be obtained by coupling the Harmonic Trumpet of an upper manual with a powerful 8′ Flute on the 1st manual, both stops being enclosed in a swell-box, and allowing the magnificent trumpet-tone or that of the quiet flute to emerge alternately by the use of the swell pedal. A similar but somewhat softer effect may be obtained by using a Clarinet and a Gedackt. (See COUPLER.)

Doppelpedal (Double Pedal). See HOHLFLÖTE.

Doppelrohrflöte. See ROHRFLÖTE.

Doublette. The name given by French builders to the stop known in German organs as Octave 2′. The French name is still found in some old Swiss and German organs. Steinmeyer has recently placed a Doublette 2⅔′ in his remarkable organ in the Gedächtniskirche in Speyer. Some builders also give the name of Doublette to a "rustling" Quint ("Rauschquinte") 2⅔′ and 2′.

Druckknöpfe. Pneumatic buttons or pistons. See PNEUMATIC PISTONS.

Dulcian. A soft-toned, bassoon-like reed, 8′ and 16′; as a rule open, but sometimes stopped. It must not be confused with the

Dulciana, a characteristic, light, string-toned stop, 8′ and 4′, of relatively large scale and, as regards power, midway between the Dolce and the Salicional. It lends itself to all kinds of combinations. It is found, among others, in the organs at Riga; in Westminster Abbey; in Notre-Dame and in the Madeleine, Paris; on the 4th manual of an organ in Murcia. The Dulciana also appears sometimes as a pedal stop. I have met with some fine Dulcianas in the Gedächtniskirche, Berlin, and in the Gürzenich organ in Cologne (both by Sauer). A Dulcianbass 16′ occurs in the Kreuzkirche, Dresden (Jehmlich), and a Salicetbass 16′ in St Michael's, Hamburg (Walcker). In Switzerland it is found as a manual stop at Zürich-Enge, Wald, Liestal, Rapperswil, Lausanne, etc. As a pedal stop of splendid effect, half Harmonica, half Salicional, in St Peter's, Leipzig; in the Berlin Cathedral; in the Stadtkirche, Esslingen; and in St Jacob's, Hamburg. The organ in the Town Hall of Heidelberg (Voit) possesses a Dulciana 8′ on the Echo manual. The Dulciana—like the Dolce and the Harmonica—renders valuable aid to the pedal department as a transmission-stop (see TRANSMISSION).

Dulcianbass. See DULCIANA.

E

Echo. When this word alone appears on the drawknob, it indicates an exceedingly soft, flute-like stop, which is often placed in a swell-box, separate from the main body of the organ (see VOX HUMANA). It is sometimes labelled Bourdon-Echo (as a rule 8′); in this capacity it is frequently employed to soften the often somewhat metallic tone of the Vox Humana. See CRESCENDO, ECHOBASS, VOX HUMANA, and TONHALLE.

Echobass 16' (or Lieblich-Gedacktbass 16') is the softest of stopped pedal pipes. It is very useful for supplying the bass in pianissimo passages by coupling it with a soft 8' stop, *i.e.* the Harmonica, the Dulciana, the Æoline, or a stop belonging to the Echo organ (see TONHALLE). I think I am correct in attributing to my dear colleague J. Luz, the excellent Zürich organist, the original idea of making use of pneumatic transmission to obtain an independent pedal stop out of the swell manual Lieblich-Gedackt 16'. This stop should never be omitted from large organs as an independent pedal stop, together with the 16' Subbass; and it has been placed, for instance, with the Harmonica 8', in quite a number of modern instruments.

In organs where this stop is not placed in a real Echo swell-box, *i.e.* where it does not serve as a transmission of such a stop, it should be described only as Lieblich-Gedacktbass. Regarding the Lieblich-Gedackt 32' as Echobass, see end of article TRUMPET.

Echocornett. See CORNET.

Echo Gamba. A solo stop frequently met with nowadays—for instance, in the Musiksaal at Vienna, and as an 8' solo stop in the swell of the organs built by Walcker for Montevideo and Shanghai. These two organs, possessing, respectively, twenty-eight and thirty-three stops, have no less than three manuals, which is very convenient for the organist, upon whom constantly increasing demands are being made.

Echomixtur (Mixtur ætherea). See HARMONICA ÆTHEREA.

Echowerk. See CRESCENDO.

Electricity. See ELECTRO-PNEUMATIC and CALCANT.

Electro-pneumatic Action. Nowadays organs are frequently met with whose component parts are placed at considerable distance from each other, as is the case, for instance, with organs at Forst, Lyon, Einsiedeln, and Genoa. This divided arrangement is rendered possible by means of the electro-pneumatic action, concerning which I may be allowed to give a few particulars. It was in the factory of F. Goll, at Lucerne, that I had the opportunity of examining one of the first systems of the kind; and I became convinced that the electro-pneumatic system was soon destined to play a great rôle in the construction of organs, and for the following reasons:—

(1) Electricity suppresses distance. Hence no more disputes between builders and committees with regard to a foot more or less of space to be allowed for the organ, since the console may be easily separated from the body of the instrument. The latter may be erected in the most convenient place, regardless of

distance, provided, of course, exigencies of acoustics are always taken into account. Communication between the keys and the valves of the pipes is established by means of an almost invisible electric cable. When the keys are depressed, the sound is heard as simultaneously as if the two portions of the instrument were united in one; and the player, placed at a certain distance from the body of the organ, will be the better able to judge the effect of his playing, and to modify it accordingly.

(2) Electricity does away with quite a lot of levers, backfalls, trackers, and other cumbersome devices, and thus lessens considerably the possibility of accidental derangements of mechanism, as well as hindrances arising from changes of temperature.

(3) The cost of maintenance will be reduced to a minimum by the use of electric batteries. The electric current is put in motion or stopped by a most simple apparatus. It goes without saying that this system does not dispense with bellows. (See VENTILATORS.) As soon as the air commences to operate upon the latter, the current is established or suppressed by a small intercalary bellows. It is of great importance that the current from the keys to the valves be established with the help of little bellows, intermediary levers; hence the name electro-pneumatic. The objection to the introduction of electro-pneumatic action on the ground of less prompt speech resulting therefrom is, with a very few exceptions, groundless.

I would mention here the Saalbau organ in Wiesbaden, also the organs at Munich, Berlin, Heidelberg, etc. I have examined several large new organs in which notable builders have made successful use of electricity.

Among the large electro-pneumatic organs which I have examined, I would mention specially that in the Church of the Immaculate Conception, at Genoa, which possesses four manuals. The console is installed behind the high altar, and the different portions of the organ are variously disposed in the church. The electro-pneumatic concert organ at Heidelberg (Voit) has a portable console, with which it is connected by means of a cable fifty metres long.

For the present, it is scarcely possible to apply generally the *purely electric* system. First of all, because it does not offer absolute guarantee of reliability; secondly, a sudden and complete transformation would involve existing factory arrangements in revolutionary modifications which require time. The *electro-pneumatic* system, on the contrary, has a great future in store.

In addition, distances may in a certain measure be surmounted by the employment of the *purely pneumatic* system. The organ in the English Church at Lucerne (Goll) is thus connected up at four corners.

Electro-pneumatic action must be employed with care, as the dispersion of sonorous bodies can bring about serious inconvenience from the point of view of acoustics. Chladni, whom Tyndall (p. 160) calls "the father of modern acoustics," has furnished some interesting particulars in his illustrated work. Compare also the remarks by A. Feith in the *Z. f. I.* with regard to regulating the speech through a sudden or gradual depression of the keys, and also as regards the Accentcoupler by Schlag (Philharmonic) for obtaining dynamic changes in the same manual through varied pressure. At Einsiedeln, Fr. Columban († 1905), abbot-superior of the convent, showed me some new and very practical applications of electricity in the construction of organs (see REED STOPS). I would refer the reader to what I have written in the article Bassoon. As is well known, Fr. Columban was a great authority on this subject. He was kind enough to furnish me with some notes upon the application of electricity to organ-building, which I transcribe herewith:—

"Electro-pneumatic action is useful for small organs only when local conditions necessitate separating the console from the main body of the instrument, or different parts from each other, and for the following reasons:—

"(1) Compressed air, which plays an important part in tubular pneumatic organs, answers all requirements, if the system employed is a good one and the builder is conscientious. To add electricity would only complicate matters and augment the chances of derangement.

"(2) To employ batteries in order to establish electric currents is to court trouble. It is better, where possible, to make use of small special dynamos operated by the same motor as puts the bellows in motion. But all such installations are expensive, and must be supervised by a skilled workman. They are therefore not to be recommended for general use.

"(3) The contacts must undergo a sufficiently energetic friction in order to remove the layer of oxide which is formed by the spark; or else they must be made of platinum. Even in this case it is wise to rub them somewhat. And, in spite of all such precautions, it is necessary to clean, from time to time, the surfaces of the contacts, which necessitates some skill. The oxidation or the wear of the contacts necessitates the employment of the feeblest possible currents. This is another fact which prevents the general adoption of the purely electric action.

"On the other hand, if the different portions of the organ must be separated from each other, electro-pneumatic action is the only one indicated. But the installation must be easily accessible, the maker an able and conscientious one; and one cannot insist too particularly upon the recommendations given above."

With reference to acoustics, see Pisco's work, *Die neueren Apparate der Akustik,* published at Vienna, which contains, among others, all the literature upon the subject of which I have treated here. The celebrated Italian scientist, Pietro Blaserna, in his work, *Die akustischen Faktoren* (p. 50), also gives interesting information upon this subject.

See also CALCANT for the production of wind by means of electric motors.

Euphonia (from the Greek εὐφωνία, a fine sound). A reed stop of very characteristic quality, resembling that of the Clarinet and of the Physharmonica. It is sometimes found as a free reed, more often as a beating reed, when it keeps better in tune. (See PHYSHARMONICA.) It lends itself to happy combinations. The Euphonia figures in many organs at Zürich, at Schaffhausen, Riga, Maastricht; and is more and more frequently found in modern organs.

In the Kaiser Wilhelm Gedächtniskirche at Berlin (Sauer) I have found on the 3rd manual a 16′ Euphonia (half Physharmonica and half Clarinet) of admirable quality, which, in combination with stops of the Echo organ, produces some quite novel effects. (See TONHALLE.)

The churches of Saint-Eustache and Saint-Sulpice, Paris, both possessed, before their restoration, Euphonias 16′ on the pedal. In Turin, again, I found a Euphonia 8′ as a manual stop.

According to Du Hamel, the first stop thus named was inserted in the organ in Beauvais Cathedral. (See also REED STOPS.)

Evacuant (from the Latin *evacuare*, to empty) is a stop by means of which the organist, on ceasing to play, can relieve the bellows of all wind-pressure.

F

Faberton (*lit.*, " blacksmith's sound "). See GLÖCK-LEINTON, CLOCHETTES.

Fagott (= Bassoon, *q.v.*). A narrow-scale stop, generally with free reeds. I have found it as 16′ under the designation of Contrafagott, both on the manuals and on the pedals, *e.g.* in the Gedächtniskirche, Berlin, in St Peter's, Leipzig, and in Brunswick Cathedral; also, under the name of Bassoon, in the Stadtkirche, Glarus; and as Fagott in the Apostelkirche at Cologne, where it lends a penetrating power to the Great manual. Finally, as Fagott-Oboe 16′ it appears on the 1st manual of an organ at Einsiedeln, with very fine effect.

Generally speaking, this stop is met with as an 8′ only in its two lower octaves; the Clarinet and the Oboe forming its continuation in the upper octaves. See also DULCIANA.

Feldpfeife 2′. A powerful flute, rich in harmonics, appearing in St Michael's, Hamburg.

Feldtrompete. See HELIKON.

Fernflöte. See FLUTE.

Fernstation. See TONHALLE.

Fifteenth. The name given in English organs to the Super-Octave.

Fistula (*Latin*). An obsolete name for a Rohrflöte. It is interesting to note that, in an eleventh-century MS. discovered by Prof. Hermann Hagen (Bongarsienne collection), this stop is mentioned, having copper pipes: *De fistulis organicis quomodo fiant. Cuprum* ("Cyprium," Kupfer) *purissimum tundendo ad summam tenuitatem extenditur—Reliquas (fistulas) ipsius ordinis sic facies ut superiores gravioris ordinis fecisti.* See in the Town Library at Berne the catalogue of MSS. by Prof. Hagen, p. 83B, 56. (See also the article "Gamba" in Dr. H. Reimann's work, *Orgelbau in frühern Mittelalter* [Leipzig, Allgemeine Musikzeitung]).

J. Seidel (*De Orgel und ihr Bau*) and S. Weippert mention a "Fistula minima" (an uncommon stop) as a kind of Flageolet, shrill in tone and (which is rare) of narrow scale, (See also SCALE.) For the etymology of "Salicis fistula," see SALICIONAL. The *Z. f. I.*, 22nd year, No. 10, contains a valuable article with reference to the old organ in the castle of Schmalkalde, with its ivory pipes, some of which are four feet in length.

I also wish to draw attention to Dr. Otto Kinkeldey's treatise, *Orgel und Klavier*, published in 1910; it gives some interesting historical and musico-scientific dates from the history of instrumental music.

Flachflöte (*lit.*, " a flat flute "). An 8′ and 4′ metal flute with large lips and shrill tone. I have found it as a 2′ stop in the organ of the Benedictine convent at Weingarten, and as a 1′ stop in the Catholic Court organ at Dresden; also as a 1′ Piccolo of wide scale and penetrating quality in St Michael's, Hamburg (Walcker).

Flageolet. A 2′ open metal stop of flute-like quality, often of wider scale and rounder but less powerful than the Octave 2′; in this capacity, the Flageolet is of great use to brighten judiciously the upper manuals. In large instruments—for instance, in the organ at Freiburg (Switzerland) — this stop is found in the swell under the name of Flageolet-Echo, and with a somewhat softer intonation. Mention should also be made here of the Weitpfeife 2′ in the pedal of the Magdeburg Cathedral organ.

Flautino. A small 2′ metal flute, often met with in the upper manuals, to which it imparts brightness. Combined with the Gemshorn 4′ in the swell, it intensifies the effect of the latter. When one of the upper manuals possesses a Lieblich-Gedackt 16′, it is advantageous to have also a Flautino 2′.

It is evident that the existence of this and similar stops (see ZARTFLÖTE 2′) of smaller and the smallest possible kind requires the presence of proportionately numerous 4′, 8′, and 16′ stops, so as to counterbalance them. (See REGISTRATION.)

Flauto Amabile. See FLÛTE D'AMOUR.

Flauto Dolce. An 8′ and 4′ wood stop (less frequently of metal). It is particularly mentioned here among the flue stops because it is used by preference as a delicate stop on the 1st manual in new German and Swiss organs. In combination with soft stops of various kinds it renders most valuable services.

In the 2nd manual of small organs — where 4′ stops are not numerous—a fine Flauto Dolce 4′ will be effective when combined with a few soft 8′ stops, such as the Æoline, the Lieblich-Gedackt, and the Voix céleste.

In this treatise the Great manual is always understood to be *the lowest* one, although in some organs *the second* manual is so termed (Vienna, Geneva, Freiburg, Paris, and elsewhere). (In English and American organs the Great manual is the *lower* in two-manual instruments, and the *second* — counting upwards—in organs of three or more manuals.—TR.)

A happy combination is that of Flauto Dolce 8′ with

Gamba 8′ or Dolce 8′. By means of coupling, it also blends agreeably with the Æoline or Salicional placed in the swell. A fine effect may again be obtained by assigning a melody to a Flauto Dolce 8′ and accompanying it with the Voix céleste or the Salicional, reinforced by a Lieblich-Gedackt 16′ and a small 4′ stop. An equally appropriate accompaniment would be furnished by the Æoline and Lieblich-Gedackt 8′. I cannot advise too strongly the tyro to study thoroughly the combinations to be obtained from the Flauto Dolce in conjunction with other stops. (See REGISTRATION.)

Flauto Major. See FLUTE.

Flauto Piccolo or Piccolo 1′. The smallest and shrillest of all metal stops (see FLAUTINO). It is met with as a 2′ stop at Heidelberg (Voit), Helsingfors (Walcker), Ulmer Garnisonskirche (Link), and as 1′ stop at Antwerp (Schyven). A wide-scale Piccolo 2′, together with a Lieblich-Gedackt 16′, used with the swell-box closed in arpeggio passages, gives an original harp-like effect.

Flauto Traverso (*It.*; *Ger.*, Traversflöte or Querflöte; *Fr.*, Flûte traversière). An over-blowing flue pipe intended to imitate the real orchestral flute. When constructed of wood, the body of the pipe is hollowed out, and in place of the ordinary slit a round opening is made, on the other side of the pipe, such as is found in the real flute for blowing into, the wind entering through an orifice a little below the mouth-hole. The Flauto Traverso is generally a 4′ and 8′ stop on the upper manuals, and, if built by a master-hand, forms a delicious solo stop. It is also (but more rarely) met with as a 16′ pedal stop (Traversenbass).

From c' the pipes of the Flauto Traverso are of double length and pierced with a small hole at the node of vibration in order to avoid a return to the foundation tones. In French organs, the Flauto Traverso, when of larger scale, is always designated Flûte Harmonique (*q.v.*).

A fine combination may be obtained by employing the Flauto Traverso with the Æoline 8′ and the Lieblich-Gedackt 8′, or with the Oboe and the Vienna Flute. If to this combination of 8′ stops is added a Lieblich-Gedackt 16′, a darker tint will result. Failing the Flauto Traverso 4′, the Flûte d'Amour 4′ or the Flauto Dolce 4′ may be employed to brighten somewhat the more sombre stops. A melody assigned to the Flauto Traverso and accompanied by a Dolce will prove charmingly effective. One should also try the charming effect of a fine Flauto Traverso or Lieblich-Gedackt enclosed in a swell-box, by weaving it artistically around a well-voiced Vox Humana, and by the further brief and judicious employment of the tremulant. To accompany this, one should employ a Lieblich-Gedacktbass 16′ slightly emphasised by the swell Æoline; and in certain places the unobtrusive blending of a very soft Lieblich-Gedacktbass 32′ with the above will produce a fine effect.

The reader is referred to what has been said concerning the 32′ stop included with this end in view in the organ in St Michael's, Hamburg (163 stops).

For the combination of the Flauto Traverso with the Physharmonica, see the latter. (See also INTONATION.)

Flötenprincipal (Flute Principal). A Principal of flute-like quality.

Flue Stops (*Ger.*, Flötenwerk, Labialpfeifen; *Fr.*, Jeux à bouche). As this designation is frequently used for a whole family of stops in contradistinction to reed stops (*q.v.*), I shall endeavour to give a concise explanation, according to the latest results of investigation, of the generation of sound in flue pipes. The peculiarity of flue pipes is that, when they are sounding, air is the generating and vibrating body. The pipe serves only to cut off the vibrating column of air from the outer atmosphere, and to regulate the vibrations. The tone is originated at the sharp edge of the mouth (*labium*, lip); a flat current of air is driven against this lip, and in splitting produces a curious noise, which may be considered as a mixture of many tones in close proximity (cp. Melde's *Acoustics*, pp. 250

et seq.). The bore of the pipe then stimulates some of those sounds which correspond to the tones peculiar to the pipe, thereby raising them to the rank of a musical note. Even the tone of a tuning-fork, if brought into close proximity with the mouth of a tube or of an organ-pipe, is strengthened, if the pitch of the said fork corresponds to one of the notes peculiar to the pipe.

Mention might be made here of a most interesting article entitled, "How is Sound generated in the Organ-pipe?" published in the *Z. f. I.* (28th year), from the pen of my late friend and colleague, Max Allihn, a clever organ-scholar and an expert in all matters concerning the organ. Allihn here proves once more that each tone corresponds to a certain depth of the opening of the pipe, and that with a certain length of the air-column a tone is generated and sounded if the resonating body is tuned to this particular tone. (With reference to the remarks on "side-beards" at the close of this article, see GAMBA.)

Fig. 1 shows the longitudinal section of a wooden flue pipe. The vibrating column of air is cut off from the outer atmosphere and regulated by the sides R R. The air coming from the wind-chest passes through the foot into the throat or air-chamber K, from which it can now escape through the narrow slit *cd*, and in being forced against the sharp edge, *ab*, of the mouth, produces the musical tone as above described.

FLUE STOPS

Fig. 2, on the other hand, is a metal flue pipe, soldered at the top, therefore "Gedackt" (*i.e.* covered or stopped). It has been purposely placed by the side of the open flue pipe, to show the physical definition given under Gedackt (*q.v.*), according to which a stopped pipe yields a note an octave deeper than does an open pipe of the same length (see fig. 1). The letters R R again indicate the tube which encloses the sounding body of air; *ab* is the above-described site where the tone originates, and FF, the foot of the pipe, standing in the sound-board and extending to the slit (see above).

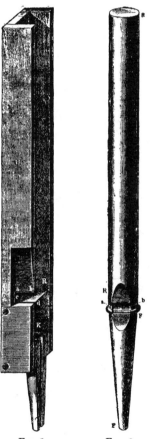

Fig. 1.   Fig. 2.

An explanation of the production of tone in flue pipes is to be found in Richter's *Catechism of the Organ*, p. 24, and in Sonrek's *Theory of the Sonorous Column of Air*.

One word more on the difficult tuning of this species of pipe. Although I am quite of the opinion, with Anding, that the tuning of flue pipes should really remain the business of the organ-builder, still I would here draw attention to the new contrivance for tuning with slots and rolled-up strips of tin (for metal pipes) or tuning sliders (for wood pipes). The main body of the pipe is made longer by half a tone than the intended pitch requires; an oblong opening, proportionate to the measurement of the pipe, is then cut in the tube just below the upper end, in such a way that its lower half begins below the actual pitch of the pipe, while the upper half extends beyond it. The strip of metal which is cut out to form the oblong opening remains attached at the lower end and is rolled up (cp. Prof. Kothe's book on organ-building, to which I am indebted for several capital illustrations). By rolling up the strip, and thereby shortening the working portion of the pipe, the pitch is sharpened; by unrolling the strip, *i.e.* lengthening the pipe, the pitch is flattened. In wood pipes the same operation is effected by means of a movable wooden slider or a flexible piece of tin-plate.

The tuning-slot gives the pipes, apart from a precise articulation, a more steady, decided tone, and adds power of expression to its qualities.

FLUE STOPS

This method of tuning must not, however, be confused with tuning-shades of older date, which served exclusively to facilitate the operation of tuning.

Fig. 3 shows the upper end of a metal pipe, on which is visible the tuning-slot a, and the strip of metal b, rolled up.

Fig. 4 shows that side of the upper end of a wood pipe at which the tuning slider a is pushed up as far over the opening b as the dotted line goes.

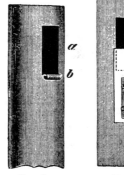

FIG. 3.   FIG. 4.

In new organ contracts, this tuning-slot arrangement is often stipulated for, particularly for the Principal Gamba stops.

Open wood pipes are tuned by means of a tuning-shade of zinc or tin-plate, bending up or down; and the metal pipes—for instance, the small mixture pipes which have no tuning-slot—are tuned by means of a tuning-cone. By narrowing the upper rim of the pipe the tone is flattened; by opening it outwards, it is sharpened.

Concerning the method of tuning stopped pipes, see GEDACKT.

Flute. When this name alone appears on the draw-knob, it refers to an open flue stop 8′ and 4′, louder than the Flauto Dolce and of wider scale. (I have found a Flauto Major as a 16′ on the Great manual of the organ at Riga.)

Flute is the generic name of a very numerous family of stops, several of which, such as Flachflöte (*q.v.*), Blockflöte, Spielflöte (in Amsterdam "Speelfluit"), Bauernflöte (*q.v.*), are seldom found in new organs. On the other hand, a Fernflöte appears in the organs at Cologne and Neuenburg (Goll); a Zartflöte in the organ at Apolda (Sauer); in the Kreuzkirche at Dresden (Jehmlich) a Holzflöte and an Offenflöte; a Flauto Eskaria (Basque Flute) in Seville Cathedral; an Orchestral Flute 4′ in the Tonhalle at Düsseldorf; a Dunkelflöte in the Passau Cathedral; and a Hellflöte in the Christuskirche at Mannheim (Steinmeyer). It is evident that, in organs of one hundred stops or more (Ulm, Paris, Liverpool, London, Sydney, Libau in Russia, Riga, Berlin, Hamburg, Garden City, and others), some names for the same or a similar stop may occur with slightly altered etymology, solely for purposes of distinction. In languages which possess a poor vocabulary, such as the Finnish, for instance, it is very difficult to translate these almost identical names. I would take this opportunity to warmly thank Prof. Merikanto, the genial organist of Helsingfors Cathedral, for the enormous trouble which he has taken in translating this small technical work into his own language. (See also CONCERT FLUTE.)

Steinmeyer, at Oettingen, has made, under the name of Tibia, a flute stop of very wide scale, which forms either an excellent solo stop or a very good "filling-up" stop, sufficiently powerful to support the Principal —thus, in the Christuskirche organ at Carlsruhe.

I shall describe, one by one, the most important representatives of the flute family, as I have already done with the Flauto Dolce. In buildings where there is but little space available for the organ, the experiment has been tried (by Walcker and others) of constructing triangular flute pipes. Large lips have also been tried in order to obtain a louder intonation.

The Flute 8′ lends itself to the same combinations as the Flauto Dolce, but it is somewhat louder than the latter. There is scarcely an organ which does not include an 8′ Flute on the pedal, under the name Bass Flute. (This is unfortunately not altogether true of *English* organs.—TR.)

As is mentioned at the end of the article Subbass, the Bass Flute—like the somewhat more powerful Bass Octave—imparts to the lower notes of the pedal not only precision—a quality particularly belonging to the Violoncello—but rather *body*; and to the upper notes of the Subbass the fullness which the latter stop so often lacks. As to the double-lipped Flute or Doppelflöte, see the article DOPPELFLÖTE.

It should be mentioned here that stops which are

naturally constructed of wood have their upper notes made of metal in order to give them more body, as, for instance, the small Gedackts.

Flûte à Cheminée. See ROHRFLÖTE.

Flûte d'Amour (Flauto Amabile). A charming wood stop of narrow scale. German builders make it of 8′ and 4′; Swiss builders, more frequently as a 4′ stop. It is well represented, under the name Flauto d'Amore 4′, in the 3rd manual of the organ in Berne Cathedral.

The Flûte d'Amour is frequently met with on the Great manual, where it replaces the Spitzflöte 4′, and, together with the Flauto Dolce 8′, renders good service as a solo stop—for instance, in St Martin's, Vevey, and in the German Church at Montreux. It lends precision to the Gedackts, whose tone is deeper, as well as to the string-toned stops (see ÆOLINE). In the excellent organs by Steinmeyer this same stop is often labelled Amorosa.

The name of Flûte d'Amour is also given to a soft metal Flauto Traverso.

Flûte Octaviante or **Flûte Harmonique.** See HARMONIC FLUTE.

Fourniture (also Plein jeu, *Fr.*). The French name for Mixture (*q.v.*).

Free Combinations. See REGISTRATION.

Frein harmonique. An invention of Gavioli, of Paris. Its scope is to impart to stops of narrow scale, such as the Gamba, Violoncello, Viola, etc.—a more pronounced "bite" and a finer tone. It is a narrow metal plate of the same length as the mouth of the pipe, fixed obliquely on an adjustable spring. I have referred (see GAMBA) to the effectiveness of this Frein, which answers even in the case of the smallest scale string stops. Sauer, the genial pupil of Cavaillé-Coll, has done much to make this contrivance known in Germany.

Fugara. This stop closely resembles the Gamba, and is midway between the latter and the Geigenprincipal, than which it is often sharper. It is made as 8′ or 4′, more rarely as 16′ (Halle a. Saale).

Jos. Dobler, in the *Grazer Z. f. I.*, derives the name Fugara from the Latin or the Provençal word "vōgăra," replacing. According to this authority, the name Fugara was employed for this stop because, in the upper manuals, it often replaces Principal and Octave.

Ernst Seifert has placed a strong-toned Fugara 4′ in the pedal department of the organs in the Liebfrauenkirche at Münster and in the Wallfahrtskirche at Kevelaer. This arrangement commends itself where a 4′ pedal reed would be too shrill.

One should combine a Fugara with a Clarinet, Æoline, Salicional, or Viola (8′ and 16′) and Geigenprincipal, together with a soft Flute or flute-like Gedackt borrowed by means of the melodic coupler from another manual in order to emphasise the melody. It is most important that all these stops acting together should without exception be enclosed in a swell-box, so that, for instance, the emerging Clarinet character on the one hand, and the Flute character of the melody on the other hand, may be separated through a judicious use of the different swell pedals and be effectively emphasised when required. In order to obtain fine dynamic effects one can blend into this combination of stops certain other stops by means of the Rollschweller (*q.v.*).

Thanks to Free Combination pistons, these combinations can fortunately be fixed beforehand, so as to be available for use when required. Thus one is able to interpret successfully the works of Max Reger.

Fusswalze. See ROLLSCHWELLER.

G

Gamba (*It.*, Viola da Gamba; *Ger.*, Kniegeige). A very characteristic stop which is now doubtlessly found as an 8′ stop on the Great manual of all organs. Large instruments possess even Gambas 16′; thus, the Riga Cathedral organ (124 speaking stops). The

Temple-du-Bas organ at Neuchâtel and that in Lausanne Cathedral each possess, on the 1st manual, Gamba 16′, 8′, and 4′. On the 3rd manual of the organ in St Paul's Church, Berlin (Sauer), I found a 16′ Gamba (enclosed) which lends itself to admirable combinations; thus, with Quintatön 8′, then with Rohrflöte 8′ and Viola 4′, and finally with Harmonic Trumpet 8′.

I would express my warmest thanks to Herr Arthur Egidi, the eminent Berlin organist and professor at the Akademisches Institut für Kirchenmusik, for the valuable information which he has been kind enough to convey to me. My grateful thanks are also due to the late Professor Robert Radecke, director of the same institution, for the kindly criticism of my work.

This stop frequently appears as a 16′ pedal stop in some of Sauer's organs. In the Evangelic Church at Warsaw I came across a 16′ Gamba voiced in such a characteristic manner that it could neither be replaced by the Violinbass 16′—which is louder—nor by the Harmonicabass 16′— which is feebler.

The Gamba 16′ is now frequently found on the pedal department of modern organs;

FIG. 5.—Gamba. Length and pitch same as Principal 8′; width (presupposing an 8′ Gamba) same as Octave 4′.

thus, in St John's, Bergen (Norway), and Christ Church, Berne.

The pedal stop which most closely resembles the Gamba 16′ is the Salicional 16′ (*q.v.*).

The tone of the Gamba is still more biting than that of the Salicional. One of the finest achievements of the art of modern organ-building is that of having succeeded in producing Gambas of a well-pronounced " bite " and at the same time capable of prompt speech (see VOICING). One must protest energetically against the manner—happily not too frequent—in which Gambas are voiced. They become, in such cases, Gemshorns or Geigenprincipals: they are no longer Gambas. A Gamba worthy of the name must never lose its characteristic tone: it must " bite "; and it must never be given a more or less neutral intonation.

In the Fraumünster at Zürich and in the old French organ at Berne, for instance, I found Gambas highly deserving of the name. Although not possessing the quality of very prompt speech, they have that discreetly hesitating something of the sympathetic old Gambas (Kniegeigen). In many old organs such charming Gambas were neutralised at renovations for the sake of securing a particularly prompt speech.

The late Pastor Max Allihn, unfortunately taken away too soon, a genial and kind friend, and who was of great help to me in the preparation of this book, gives, at the end of his article (*Z. f. I.*, 28th year), some interesting details with regard to the different contrivances for the improvement of the speech of pipes, based, in part, upon the vibroscopic observations made by Van Schaik upon the vibrating air-wave.

The pipes of the Gamba have a narrow mouth (*Aufschnitt*) and scale, and are therefore longer than those of the Principal and Salicional. The length of the C pipe is 8′ 3″. The scale of the Gamba 8′ is the same as that of the Octave 4′, and consequently a whole octave lower than that of the Principal.

The pipes of the Gamba, like those of the Principal and Violoncello, are made preferably of good English tin. A conical Gamba is called Spitzgambe (*Fr.*, Gambe à fuseau; *Eng.*, Cone Gamba). In examining an organ recently, in the capacity of expert, I found the lower pipes of this stop constructed of wood, according to a stipulation in the contract, and placed horizontally for reasons of space, without the quality of the tone suffering thereby. In Spanish organs, whole rows of pipes are placed horizontally—for instance, those of the Tromba (see FELDTROMPETE). Similarly placed pipes are to be seen in the Convent church at Einsiedeln. Quite recently, Aquilino Amézua has made a similar disposition of pipes in the excellent organ in Seville Cathedral (seventy-two speaking stops).

By constructing Gambas of larger scale, as is sometimes done, a more powerful tone is obtained, but a less pronounced "bite" (see above). This means renouncing the character proper of the Gamba. It can only be recommended if the organ contain a Viola to fill up the gap which inevitably results. See above for what has been said upon this important subject.

A good Gamba does not require to be accompanied by any other stop. Nevertheless, in cases where the colouring produced by the flutes should be deemed advantageous, I would recommend the employment of a well-voiced Gedackt, a Hohlflöte, a Rohrflöte, and a Flûte d'Amour. A well-made, cutting Gamba 8′ accompanied by a Bourdon 8′ and Octave 4′ gives almost the effect of a reed stop. (See REGISTRATION.)

The Gamba, like all string-toned stops, such as the Æoline, Viola, and Salicional, lends itself to studies in registration and tone-colour (*Klangfarbenstudien*), which I commend to the beginner to carry out in the manner already indicated in the article ÆOLINE.

As regards pipes to be placed in the interior, one can perfectly well mix a small quantity of lead with the tin (see below); this is done in practice.

For the history of the construction of organ-pipes and the materials employed therein (see also FISTULA) the reader is referred (among others) to Wangemann's work. The words "pure English tin," "Probezinn," and "metal" often employed in organ-building parlance, indicate the different proportions of lead which enter into the tin in the construction of pipes. In new organs a harder metal is employed, which is called "spotted metal."

These various compositions are distinguished as follows:—pure English tin (in which is reckoned also the so-called 15 half-oz. tin), proportion 1 : 15; the common English tin, proportion 2 : 14; Probezinn, proportion 4 : 12; and metal, which contains $\frac{1}{3}$, often $\frac{1}{2}$, of lead. It would be interesting to furnish other chemical details regarding tin and its various alloys, but this would lead us beyond the scope of this book.

It is evident, besides, that the proportions which I have just given are more or less subject to modification, according to the customs of different builders and to the contracts made with them. Professors Hornik and Jörázek, of Prague, refer in the *Z. f. I.* to successful organ-pipes with solderless tubes, the work of S. Petr, of Prague.

For the front pipes pure tin only should be employed if means allow it, even if the original estimate should be somewhat increased thereby. For, instead of the silvery shimmer (see PRINCIPAL) which forms the chief decoration of organ fronts, a somewhat bluish tint or, in worse cases, oxide of lead spots show up only too soon where an alloy is used.

On the subject of the materials employed in the construction of organ-pipes and their influence upon tone, see also Zamminer, *Die musikalischen Instrumente in ihren Beziehungen zur Akustik* ("Musical Instruments in their relation to Acoustics"), pp. 261 *et seq.*; also Professor Schafhäutl's *Versuch mit Metall,*

Holz und Pappe ("Experiments with Metal, Wood, and Pasteboard"). (See also REED STOPS.)

Here are some interesting details concerning "spotted metal," now so frequently employed. This is an alloy of tin and lead. By employing 52 per cent. of tin one obtains smaller spots; by using 48 per cent., larger spots are obtained. It is for the architects to say what they require, the organ front assuming a different aspect accordingly. It is important that entirely new metal be used for this alloy, old metal showing up unfavourably after recasting.

For some time past considerable use has been made of zinc in the construction of organ-pipes, and that with perfect success. Thus, at the present day, when architects often require a duller tone for organ-fronts in modern buildings, the front pipes are made preferably in bronze-aluminium. Nevertheless, the slot, the lips, the tuning strips, and the foot of the pipe should be made of English tin, which is easier to work.

New studies and experiments are continually being made relative to the materials employed in organ-pipes. I am keeping myself carefully informed of all these novelties; and organ-builders will greatly oblige me if, on their part, they will be good enough to inform me of any new development along this line.

Gambenbass (Bass Gamba). See GAMBA.

Gebläsemotoren (Wind Motor). See CALCANT.

Gedackt or Gedeckt (*lit.*, "stopped"; *Fr.*, Bourdon, *q.v.*). Stopped pipes, 4′, 8′, 16′, and 32′. In wooden pipes the top is "stopped" by a kind of leather-covered plug (fig. 6); in metal pipes, by a metal cap (fig. 7).

The family of stopped pipes is one of the most

FIG. 6.   FIG. 7.

important in the organ: all the Bourdons and the Subbass are included therein. German builders employ a great variety of names according to the power and the scale: the Lieblich-Gedackt (*Fr.*, Bourdon aimable); the Sanft-Gedackt (soft Bourdon); the Still-Gedackt (still Gedackt); the Zart-Gedackt (tender Gedackt); the Gross-Gedackt (Grand Bourdon); and the Grob-Gedackt (*lit.*, coarse Gedackt).

In the concert organ in the Liederhalle at Stuttgart (Weigle) I found a Gross-Gedackt 8′ on reinforced air-pressure (see TUBA MIRABILIS). Some builders construct the Lieblich-Gedackt 8′ with double lips from g. See also BOURDON.

A fine Lieblich-Gedackt, made by a master and enclosed in a swell-box (*q.v.*), is one of the most exquisite stops of the organ. It permits the discreet employment of the Tremolo, and an able organist can obtain some charming effects from it. For Gedackts on the pedal, see SUBBASS.

Every stopped pipe may be considered as an open pipe cut off at the node of vibration (Töpfer). It sounds an octave lower than an open pipe of the same length, because, in stopped pipes, the sound-waves, as soon as they have reached the bottom of the pipe, return upon themselves and continue in this new direction, so that they cover the same amount of space as in an open pipe of double length. Stopped pipes of large scale, when blown feebly, yield an almost pure foundation-tone; in those of narrow scale the twelfth is distinctly heard (Helmholtz). See QUINTATÖN.

A double-lipped Gedackt (see DOPPELFLÖTE) gives a clearer and more powerful tone than a single-lipped one. The English call "Stopped" what the Germans call "Gedackt"; thus, their "Stopped Diapason 8′" corresponds to the Gedackt 8′. An organ of any importance ought in all cases to have a Lieblich-Gedackt 16′ on the swell, as well as in the Tonhalle (*q.v.*), and this for the same reasons which I urged in favour of the presence of the Bourdon 16' on the 1st manual. Excellent effects may be obtained by combining the Lieblich-Gedackt with the Voix céleste in the upper octaves. See also BOURDON and VOIX CÉLESTE.

Together with my friend Luz, I would recommend a Lieblich-Gedacktbass 16' (Echobass 16') for the pedal department of large organs. This stop, combined with the Harmonicabass 8', furnishes an appropriate bass for soft stops (as regards 32', see end of article). It is doubtless with the same intention that Prof. Dr. Wolfrum has had placed in the Stadthalle at Heidelberg a soft Gedacktbass 16' as an independent pedal stop, in addition to a Subbass 16'.

Under the name of Gedacktflöte (stopped flute) 8' and 4' is often designated a stopped pipe of narrow scale and of flute character. A Gedeckt minor 4' is found in the Barfüsser Church at Augsburg. (Notice the spelling of the word *Gedeckt* on this occasion. This is the *correct* spelling for the German word; *Gedackt* is almost universally tolerated in the designation of organ-stops; *Gedacht*, however, is *wrong*.—TR.)

The Gedackts add body to the foundation stops, and they are employed where it is desired to lend a fuller and darker tone to combinations. (See BOURDON and REGISTRATION.) But the constant employment of Gedackts in the rendering of polyphonic compositions, with their dissonances, would result in a lack of colour, strength, and precision (Helmholtz).[1] See also KLANGFARBE.

In order to tune stopped pipes (see FLUE PIPES)—and this should always be done by the builder himself—the plug or the cap is drawn up or pushed down. In the first procedure the pipe is lengthened and the tone is flattened; in the second the pipe is shortened and the tone is accordingly sharpened. With reference to the combination of a Lieblich-Gedacktbass 32′ enclosed in a swell-box with other 32′ stops, see my remarks at the end of the article TRUMPET.

Gedacktbass (Stopped Bass). This 8′ pedal stop renders acceptable service for soft accompaniments. It is found, for instance,—in addition to a Subbass 16′ and an Octavebass 8′—on the pedal of the organ at Kwassitz (Bros. Rieger). With the same object in view, Walcker has similarly placed in the organ at Kotka (Finland) a very soft Gedacktbass 16′, in addition to the Subbass 16′. The same builder has placed a Gross-Gedacktbass 32′ in the swell of the organ in St Michael's, Hamburg. See ECHOBASS and end of article TRUMPET.

Gedacktflöte. See GEDACKT.

[1] Pietro Blaserna, *Theorie des Schalls* ("Theory of Sound") (Leipzig), p. 203, considers that harmonics are indispensable for the individualisation of musical sounds.

Gedacktquint. See QUINT.

Gedeckt minor. See GEDACKT.

Geigenprincipal (Violin Principal). A metal stop of very narrow scale found nowadays in nearly all fair-sized instruments. It is found as 8′ and 4′, much more rarely as a 16′ (Garnisonskirche, Berlin; and in the 2nd manual of the organs in St Paul's, Hamburg; Nicolai, Libau; and St John's, Helsingfors). It has a "biting" tone which recalls that of the violin. It is placed on one of the secondary manuals, where it plays the rôle of the Great Principal. Narrow-scaled pipes sound distinctly a certain number of harmonics in addition to the foundation-tone. Such is the case, for instance, with the Geigenprincipal, the Violoncello, the Violonbass, Viola da Gamba, etc. It is precisely to their harmonics that, according to Helmholtz, these stops owe their characteristic tone (see *Die Lehre von den Tonempfindungen*, p. 151). On the contrary, if the scale is wide, the pipe can stand a sufficiently strong pressure of air without yielding harmonics; the fundamental tone is heard strong and full, and the harmonics are feeble. Such is the case with the Diapasons, which, for this reason, constitute the fundamental stops of the organ. When the Geigenprincipal appears on the swell it represents a normal and healthy tone, more conforming to the nature of the organ than certain characteristic stops which are often the result of artificiality. As an 8′ stop, it blends perfectly, like the Salicional, with the Gemshorn 4′ in rapid passages.

One should try Clarinet 8′, Æoline 8′, Salicional (or Viola) 8′ and 16′, and Geigenprincipal, emphasising the melody by a fine flute borrowed by means of the melodic coupler (all these stops being enclosed in a swell-box), and allow the flute, string, or reed tone to emerge judiciously according to requirement. In certain music by Reger, and in Wagner transcriptions, this combination produces an orchestral effect. See also REGISTRATION and KLANGFARBE.

American builders give the name of "Violin Diapason" to the Geigenprincipal.

Gemischte Stimmen (*lit.*, "mixed voices"). See MIXTURE.

Gemshorn (*Fr.*, "Cor de chamois"). A metal stop, with conical pipes, something like those of the Principal. It is slightly more powerful than the Geigenprincipal, and its tone recalls that of the Horn. It is found as 8′ and 4′. In old organs it sometimes differs in tone, being more mellow and of very slight cutting quality. In this form it lends itself admirably in the interpretation of Bach's "Choralvorspiele" and other analogous compositions. A Gemshorn 4′, of clear and singing quality, accompanied by a Geigenprincipal 8', a Lieblich-Gedackt 16', and placed in the swell, is admirably effective.

In the new organ at The Hague I have found a Gemshorn 2'. The organ in Westminster Abbey possesses a Harmonic Gemshorn 2' (see also FLAUTINO). The Gürzenich organ at Cologne (Sauer) possesses a Gemshorn 16' on the pedal, provided with "beards." On the pedal department of the new organ in Berlin Cathedral, also by Sauer, I have found a Gemshorn 16' which, as regards tone, is between a Salicional and a Subbass; the same in the Jerusalem organ. In the organ in Christ Church, Mannheim (Steinmeyer), are to be found an 8' and a 4' Gemshorn, both labelled Silbermann Mensur. Elsewhere in this book I have referred to the ever-increasing influence of Silbermann's scales and voicing, and have added some examples.

Gemshornquinte. See QUINT.

Generalcoppel (General Coupler) (see also COLLECTIVE COUPLER). A draw-stop which allows the simultaneous employment of all the couplers (*e.g.* Heidelberg). In an organ at Speyer (Steinmeyer) it appears under the name *Totalcoppel*.

Generalcrescendo or Registerschweller. See CRESCENDO.

Gleichschwebende Temperatur (Equal Temperament). See OCTAVE.

Glockenspiel. See CARILLON.

Glöckleinton 2′ (*Fr.* Clochettes 2′). A stop which is still met with nowadays in large instruments, *e.g.* in the interesting organ in Schneeberg (Saxony) Cathedral. It is doubtless the same stop as the *Faberton* which I have found mentioned in an old MS. organ-specification in the archives of the convent at Einsiedeln. It probably imitated the sound of the smith's (*Faber*) hammer beating upon the anvil. The MS. is dated 1557, and it is the work of the builder Balthasar Mygeln of Basle. (See also FISTULA, and the note at the conclusion of the article.)

It would carry me beyond the scope of this book to collect all the names of the old stops from this or that archive and compare them with the nomenclature and character of our modern stops. We therefore owe much to the Bernese scholar, Dr. Adolf Fluri, for the valuable and original information concerning organ-contracts (*Orgelschlagen*) in olden times, which he has made public in his contributions to the history of the organ.

Grand Bourdon. See QUINT.

Great Quint. In English organs, the Quint $10\frac{2}{3}′$.

Gross-Cymbel. See CYMBAL.

Grossgedacktbass. See GEDACKT.

Grossmixtur. See MIXTURE.

H

Harmonica 8′. A very soft stop of the Gamba family, of narrow scale, stronger than the Æoline but less powerful than the Salicional. It is a fine solo stop. It is generally found on the 2nd or 3rd manual of large organs (*e.g.* at Frankfurt a. M., Wesel, Ulm, Leipzig, Berne, Lucerne). At Frankfurt a. Oder it is labelled Flöte Harmonica 8′, and in Canterbury Cathedral it is called Harmonic Flute 4′.

I have found on the pedal of the Fraumünster organ at Zürich a particularly successful Harmonica 8′ with metal pipes; and here I would once more express my thanks to my colleague, Herr Musikdirektor Luz, for the copious information with which he has furnished me in the preparation of this new edition of my work. (See also HARMONIC FLUTE.) This stop is useful on the pedal to lend precision to the Lieblich-Gedackt 16′. For this reason I advised its adoption in the rebuilding of the organ in Berne Cathedral. For further details concerning the use of this stop as a pedal stop, see HARMONICABASS.

Where financial considerations do not allow an independent Harmonicabass 8′, one should endeavour to obtain its equivalent by means of "borrowing," through a manual Dolce or something analogous. The Harmonica is the softest stop of the Echo organ (Fernwerk), and of charming effect. One should combine, for instance, a Harmonica 8′ with a Still-Gedackt 16′ in the upper octaves of the swell, allowing, at times, a Fernflöte with Tremulant to emerge on another manual.

One must not confuse the Harmonica either with the Physharmonica (*q.v.*) or with certain mutation stops, such as the Progressio Harmonica (Lübeck; Grafenrheinfeld; Merseburg; Liederhalle, Stuttgart; Garnisonskirche, Ulm) and Harmonica ætherea (Echo manual of the organ in the Cathedral at Riga; the large organ at Wesel; Christ Church, Berne; Heidelberg Stadthalle; Nicolaikirche, Leipzig). These two latter stops figure on the upper manuals as kinds of Echo-mixtures, mostly of three ranks and of Gamba scale.

With reference to what is known as *chemische Harmonica*, important from the point of view of experiments on the production of sound in organ-pipes, see Melde's *Akustik*, § 80. My thanks are also due to this scholar for the information with which he has been kind enough to furnish me.

Harmonica ætherea. See HARMONICA.

Harmonicabass. An extremely light and slightly "stringy" pedal stop, constructed of wood, generally

16′, more rarely 8′. It is practically of the same strength as the Salicetbass or the Salicional 16′ (*q.v.*). It forms an excellent bass for soft passages, and, in this capacity, blends with the Lieblich-Gedackt 16′ or Subbass 16′ (*q.v.*). Walcker has placed in the pedal of the 5th manual of the organ in St Michael's, Hamburg, a Contra-Harmonicabass 32′ with stopped wood pipes of slightly stringy tone, which, used with string and Gedackt stops, produces an effect of rare beauty.

By means of coupling, one can also combine the Harmonicabass with a Lieblich-Gedackt 16′ or 8′ placed in the swell. For transmission (borrowing), see ECHOBASS. All large organs should contain a Harmonicabass; it is to the pedal what the Æoline is to the manual. (See ÆOLINE, ÆOLIANBASS, and HARMONICA.)

Harmonicaflöte. See HARMONICA and MELOPHONE.

Harmonic Flute (*Fr.*, Flûte Harmonique). This stop is found in all French organs. It is an "overblowing" flute, 8′ or 4′, of large scale and with metal pipes. It is also met with in organs of other nations. Sauer, for instance, has placed it on the 1st manual of the Gedächtniskirche, where it is very effective. This same stop occurs as Harmonieflöte 8′ in the excellent organ in the Reformed Church, Leipzig, built by Furtwängler & Hammer, of Hanover; this

Harmonieflöte is constructed like the Harmonic Flute. In the higher octaves it is "over-blowing," with metal pipes of large scale.

When of narrow scale, the Harmonic Flute 8′ is called "Flûte Traversière" in French organs; when it appears as 4′, it is called "Flûte Octaviante." I would express here my profound gratitude to my colleague and friend Luz, of Zürich, a learned scholar, who has furnished for this work (and especially for this article) some useful information.

Harmonic stops, so called because they are based upon the employment of harmonics, play an important part in French organs; they constitute as much as a sixth part of an instrument.

M. Adrien de la Fage, in his report to the Société des Beaux-Arts of Paris (p. 75 *et seq.*), gives some interesting notes regarding harmonics, and refers to their employment in organ-building in France.

Frédéric Ladegast writes as follows regarding the harmonics of pipes (Töpfer, vol. ii. § 619):—"As is well known, these sounds possess a degree of power and fullness not possessed by those of ordinary pipes yielding only the foundation-tone. The column of air of pipes producing harmonics is divisible into two, three, four, or more vibrating portions. The sound is richer; it is reinforced without becoming shrill, and the whole scale becomes more even." I might mention here an appliance which I have found in the factory of Cavaillé-Coll (Paris), and which Dienel has described in *Urania*, 35th year, No. 12. This appliance shows the effect of harmonics upon the foundation-tone, while their name, number of sonorous vibrations per second, and length in metres are recorded on a chart.[1] See also KLANGFARBE.

For the designation "harmonic" as applied to reed stops, see HARMONIC TRUMPET.

Harmonic Trumpet (*Ger.*, Harmonietrompete; *Fr.*, Trompette harmonique). As applied to reed stops, the term "harmonic" (*i.e.* "over-blowing") is a misnomer. The term, as here employed, refers to the fact that this stop, in its upper octaves, is furnished with a bell double the ordinary length—in the case of the Harmonic Trumpet, generally starting from *c*. The object of this bell is to reinforce the volume of sound, which tends to become enfeebled as the sounds ascend, and thus out of proportion to that of the lower octaves. The organs in Saint-Sulpice in Paris and in the Kaiser Wilhelm Gedächtniskirche, Berlin, for instance, possess a good Harmonic Trumpet 8′.

In the organ of the English Church at Clarens (Kuhn) and in the Berne Casino organ (Goll) this stop

[1] See also p. 211 of Pietro Blaserna's work, which treats upon this subject. Blaserna says that König has constructed a similar appliance (see fig. 36 in his work) founded upon Helmholtz's principle of resonating bodies. This appliance consists of eight resonating bodies united by elastic membranes acting upon very mobile gas flames. It demonstrates that all musical instruments produce harmonics, and, further, it indicates the harmonic series.

is found both on the Great and on the swell (see SWELL). See also FLÛTE HARMONIQUE and TRUMPET.

Harmonieflöte. See HARMONIC FLUTE.

Harmonium. See PHYSHARMONICA.

Helikon 16'. A high-pressure stop, called by Allihn Feldtrompete, placed horizontally. In St Michael's, Hamburg (Walcker), it appears on the 3rd manual. At Dortmund are to be found horizontal Feldtrompeten. In Spanish organs horizontal pipes are very frequently met with.

Hellflöte (*lit.*, "a light flute"). See FLUTE.

Hochdruckluft-Register (High-pressure Stops). See TUBA MIRABILIS.

Hohlflöte (*Fr.*, Flûte creuse; *lit.*, "a hollow flute"). An open, wide-scaled flute, constructed of wood, and of full and pleasing intonation. It is generally found on the manuals as 2', 4', and 8'; under the name of Quintflöte and Hohlquinte it appears also as Quint $5\frac{1}{3}'$, $2\frac{2}{3}'$, and $1\frac{1}{3}'$. As a 1' stop it is called Sifflöte, and as 16', Grosshohlflöte. I have found a Hohlflöte 2' on the pedal of the Ulm Cathedral organ—a rare occurrence. In combination with other well-chosen stops, it imparts to the pedal, without the necessity of employing a coupler, a power of expression which ordinarily belongs only to the manuals. Before its restoration this organ possessed two pedal-boards. The same with the organs in St Paul's, Frankfurt a. M.; Marienkirche, Lübeck; Stiftskirche, Stuttgart. Nowadays, thanks to combination pedals and buttons and to the coupling mechanisms, which are so useful, two pedal-boards are unnecessary. Even for the 163-stop organ in St Michael's, Hamburg, only one pedal-board has been provided. (See also PEDAL-COLLECTIVEN.)

The Hohlflöte 4' and the Gamba 8' form a happy combination, whose tone recalls that of the Horn. The Hohlflöte also blends agreeably with the Geigenprincipal 8' placed in the swell; also with a fine Gamba 4'. On the 3rd manual of the organ built by Sauer in the Gedächtniskirche, Berlin, I have found a very fine Hohlflöte 8', which lends itself admirably to the above-named combinations. The organs at Aarau and at Berne (both by Goll) each possess a fine Hohlflöte 4'.

Holzflöte (*lit.*, "a wooden flute"). See FLUTE.

Holzmaterial (*lit.*, "wood-material"). See Reed Stops.

Horn 8'. This stop is found in the organ at Einsiedeln as a high-pressure stop. It has a tendency to over-blow. Its mellow and agreeable tone recalls the instrument of the same name. This tone is due to a special manner of constructing the reeds, the tuning-wires, and the bells. (See what is said concerning high-pressure stops at the end of the article TUBA MIRABILIS.)

In the 3rd manual of the Brunswick Cathedral organ (Furtwängler & Hammer) I have found a Horn 8′ of rare beauty, its scale being wider than that of an English Horn, and of a rather full tone, in strength resembling a soft Trumpet. Brindley & Foster have placed a Horn 8′ on the swell of the Pietermaritzburg (Natal) organ. A Horn 4′ also appears as the 163rd stop in the specification of the gigantic organ in St Michael's, Hamburg.

I

Intonation (from the Latin *intonare*, "to sound," or "cause to sound"). See VOICING.

J

Jubalflöte, so named after Jubal, the father of Music, according to the Old Testament (Gen. iv.). It is a double-lipped, open flute of strong and clear intonation, bearing a close resemblance to the Doppelflöte. I have found this stop as 8′ on the 1st manual of the organ in St Paul's, Frankfurt a. M.; and under the name Doppelflöte (*q.v.*), also 8', in some of Weigle's organs. It is rarely found as 4' and 2'. In the organ in St Mary's, Lübeck, it is a double-lipped Gedackt 8'. I have said elsewhere that the Jubalflöte or the Doppelflöte brightens agreeably the tone of a fine Gamba. It has been placed as a high-pressure stop in St Michael's, Hamburg.

K

Keraulophon (from the Greek κεραύλης, "the horn-player"). A flue stop after the manner of the Geigenprincipal. It has a delicate tone, recalling that of the Horn, and is often met with in large modern organs: Roosevelt (New York) has placed it in the 115-stop organ at Garden City; Steinmeyer, in the Frauenkirche organ at Munich; William Hill (London), in the Westminster Abbey organ and on the choir manual of the Queen's Hall organ; Musson, in a Nottingham organ; and Merklin in the Saint-Eustache organ, Paris. The employment of this stop is becoming more general.

Klangfarbe (*Ger.*; *lit.*, "tone-colour"; *Fr.*, timbre. There is no English equivalent for this admirable German word.—TR.). This expression, to denote the characteristic quality, or, as the French say, the "timbre," of a sound, is found on nearly every page throughout this book, and is used in connection with the external effects of the various stops of the organ, and therefore a more detailed explanation of the term is here deemed advisable. It is obvious that we cannot confuse a note given out by, say, an Oboe with the same note as played by a Flute, or the note of a Trumpet with the same note as played by a Violoncello. The character peculiar to an instrument is precisely what is termed its "Klangfarbe" or "timbre."

The German term "Klangfarbe" has become classic, so to speak, in the language of musical science, since its employment by the great acoustician Helmholtz in his work, *Tonempfindungen* (see Melde, *Akustik*, p. 345). The English physicist Tyndall confesses that his own language has no word to correspond exactly to the German "Klangfarbe," and envies the German language for the cleverness with which it adapts itself to the requirements of nature.

Optical science teaches us that colours result from the celerity of the vibrations of luminous waves, so that between blue and red, for instance, there exists the same relation as between a grave and an acute sound. Thus Tyndall, with whom I corresponded, rightly compares simple or fundamental colours, which offer but one number of vibrations, to simple sounds,[1] whilst all composite colours correspond

---

[1] Every compound sound, such as those produced by a string, can be divided into a series of simple sounds all belonging to the harmonic series, 1, 2, 3, 4, 5, 6. See Pietro Blaserna, *Theorie des Schalls*, p. 200.

to sounds resulting from the union of a foundation-tone with the harmonics which characterise it. It is on account of this analogy that the Germans speak of tone-colour (Klangfarbe). Helmholtz explains by this theory the characteristic tone of the Geigenprincipal. Certain stops owe their special tone to the fact that their upper harmonics are stronger than their lower ones. But the necessary basis of all harmony is furnished by what is aptly termed the "principal" stop (= English Diapason), which forms the starting-point of all other stops. The organ has this advantage over all other instruments, viz. that the player can mix or modify the tone-colour according to the pieces played (Helmholtz). A number of combinations are thus available for an able musician, even in an organ containing but a small number of stops. The organist will therefore be amply rewarded by a careful study of the tone of each of the stops contained in his organ ; he will soon acquire facility in blending them—an acquisition upon which he will congratulate himself. See what has been said in the article ÆOLINE regarding the manner of studying, and consult further the articles REGISTRATION, SALICIONAL, COUPLER, SWELL-BOX, and PROLONGEMENT.

Klaviertisch-Anlage or **Spieltisch-Anlage.** Console. See DRAW-KNOBS.

Klein-Cornett (Small Cornet). See CORNETT.

Kleingedackt (Small Gedackt). See GEDACKT.

Kleinprincipal (Small Principal). Occurs as a 4′ stop on the 2nd manual of the organ in the Heidelberg Stadthalle.

Kornett. See CORNETT.

Krummhorn. See CORMORNE.

L

Labialoboe. See OBOE.

La Force. A rare designation for a mixture which I have found in the organ of the Convent at Weingarten and in the Church of Ravensburg (Weigle). It is a five- or six-rank mixture of particularly strong intonation. Its special characteristic is that the foundation-tone is heard very distinctly, whilst the quints and tierces are much feebler—a fact which imparts to it the character of a foundation-stop rather than of a mutation stop proper. It is of very powerful effect in the fortissimo.

Larigot. An obsolete term to denote a sharp Quint $1\frac{1}{3}'$, of large scale.

Lettering (*Ger.*, Aufschriften; *Fr.*, Inscriptions). Inscriptions on draw-knobs, tilting-tablets, and plates of all sorts are, even if only something external, not unimportant in a good presentation of the complicated modern console. The player should be enabled to see at first glance, by means of appropriate colours, form, and disposition, which are speaking stops, which simply auxiliary stops, couplers, etc. Some such plan should be called for when drawing up the specification, and subsequently submitted for approval by an expert. See SPECIFICATION.

Lieblich - Gedackt (*Fr.*, Bourdon aimable). See BOURDON and GEDACKT.

M

Majorbass. This stop is now more frequently than heretofore made as a 32′ stop, *i.e.* in the Görlitz concert organ, where it is placed with an Untersatz 32′ and a Posaune (Trombone) 32′.

Manual. I deem it indispensable for every organ —even the smallest—to possess two manuals. (See SWELL-BOX and UNDA MARIS.) In the case of very large organs, where space and means allow it, I would prefer, instead of pneumatic or electric transmissions, three or even four independent manuals, thus enabling the player to interpret his intentions more adequately.

Materials employed in organ-construction. See FISTULA, GAMBA, and REED PIPES.

Melodia 8′ and **Double Melodia** 16′. Flutes with wooden pipes, akin to the Flauto Dolce, frequently met with in recently constructed English and American organs. The Melodica 8′, which is found in the Riga Cathedral organ, is another name for the same stop. The use of the Melodia in modern organs is becoming more frequent.

Melodic Coupler (*Ger.*, Melodiecoppel; *Fr.*, Accouplement mélodique). By means of this contrivance, which can be easily introduced in all pneumatic organs, one can define dynamically the melody of the Flute groups of an upper manual by means of a cutting Gamba on the 1st manual, or *vice versa*. I have found such a Double Melodic Coupler, for instance, in the two-manual Nyderck organ (Berne), rebuilt by Goll; this arrangement affords the organist a third manual for lending precision from time to time. The small extra cost of a second melodic coupler should not, therefore, be grudged. One should also try to lend additional interest to the melody of a solemn Voix céleste (*q.v.*) combination by means of a soft Dolce or Lieblich-Gedackt 8′ (with the judicious use of the tremulant for a few bars) capable of dynamic treatment. It is true that the use of a melodic coupler for a beginner is often not an unmixed blessing, for the melody should be kept completely even in order to prevent ungraceful skips. It is evident that much variety may be obtained by a judicious use of the now generally employed melodic coupler.

On the subject of auxiliary registers, I have lately had the opportunity of personally examining and approving some most convenient contrivances, the result of the inventions and increased ability of the organ-builders of all countries—for instance, in Holland, and just lately in Hanover and Brunswick, in the organ factories of Furtwängler & Hammer. The beautiful Brunswick Cathedral organ, which has been built with great skill, contains a Great to pedal coupler, which makes it possible for the pedal to play on the 1st manual. As to the advisability of this contrivance views differ, on purely technical grounds Opinion, however, is unanimous respecting the tonal worth of this work of art, which I have personally proved stop by stop. The memory will never fade of that consecrated evening hour, when, in company with the builder, who came over with me from Hanover, I listened, by the side of the Henry the Lion memorial, to the masterly playing of the Cathedral Cantor.

Melophone (from the Greek μέλος, melody, and φωνή, voice) 8′ and 4′. A delicate solo stop which is met with chiefly in Belgian and Dutch organs, *e.g.* in the swell of the organ in Notre-Dame, Antwerp. The organ in Averbode Abbey, Belgium, possesses a melophone on the pedal and on each of its four manuals. The same obtains in the organ in St Martin's, Bolsward (Low Countries).

In certain German and English organs a similar stop is found under the name of Harmonic Flute.

Membrane. See PNEUMATIC.

Metal. See GAMBA.

Mixture (*Ger.*, Mixtur (from the Latin *mixtura*); *Fr.*, Fourniture; *Ital.*, Ripieno; *Eng.*, often Sharp Mixture). The theorist is inclined to reject the idea of a contrivance by which the higher harmonic fifths and thirds, sounding with each foundation-tone, must bring hideous dissonances into every harmonious weft. Practical reasons, however, compel organist and organ-builder to retain these Mixtures. Their purpose is to produce harmonics which exist in a lesser degree in the foundation-stops of the organ than, for instance, in the instruments of an orchestra, which latter, therefore, requires artificial harmonics much less than does the organ. I disapprove of the fact that the mixture pipes are often too narrow, and thus fail in their aim. This should be noted when contracting with an organ-builder.

Even the orchestra, according to Dienel, cannot

MIXTURE

quite do without artificial harmonics, considering that the strengthening by unisons and octaves is nothing more or less than the skilful utilisation of harmonics, such as the 4′ and 2′ stops of the organ produce.

Well-composed Mixtures, supported by a practical arrangement of stops, and correctly employed, are a most effective addition to musical resources. In order to prevent the Mixture from being intolerably harsh, it is necessary to strengthen proportionately the lower tones of each note by other stops (Helmholtz, p. 98). It is on this account that, in small organs with insufficient covering, the Mixture jars, owing to the excess of harmonics (see OCTAVE). The Mixture often "breaks" (see CORNETT) in the upper octaves. The five-rank Mixture, for instance, based on C, is composed of c (4′), g ($2\frac{2}{3}′$), c (2′), g ($1\frac{1}{3}′$), c (1′); or of g ($2\frac{2}{3}′$), c (2′), g ($1\frac{1}{3}′$), c (1′), g ($\frac{2}{3}′$); the four- and three-rank Mixtures are reduced accordingly by one or two ranks. The Walkenburg organ (Klais) possesses a three- to four-rank Mixture labelled Mixturcornett.

In order to lend greater volume and power to the Mixture, particularly in the absence of a Cornet, and if the foundation-tones are not sufficiently represented, the Tierce is added; but not as the highest tone, as in the Cornet, but rather in the middle register, as in the case in Sharp (*i.e.* in the Catholic Church, Berne, where it has six ranks in the upper octaves). Several organ-builders write me that they always employ the Tierce in the Mixture, and by so doing obtain a more uniform effect; others use a Septième (Seventh) as well, nowadays. The Mixtures afford, besides, ample opportunities to organ-builders for their own special experiments and appliances.

The Mixture stop (often labelled Progressio), particularly in German organs (quite in half the cases), is built "through," that is to say, with no "breaks," and as such is generally of from two to five ranks, composed respectively of $2\frac{2}{3}'$ and $2'$; of $4'$, $2\frac{2}{3}'$, and $2'$; and, finally, of $8'$, $5\frac{1}{3}'$, $4'$, $2\frac{2}{3}'$, and $2'$ (examples in Switzerland: Engelberg Convent (Goll), and St John's, Schaffhausen (Kuhn)).

In St Michael's, Hamburg, Walcker has placed on the 1st manual a seven-rank Grossmixtur with a total number of 427 pipes.

The Mixture is no good without sufficient foundation-tones, because it contains the loud-sounding harmonics; it belongs, therefore, to the Great organ only, and has no right to be ever used separately. On the other hand, the great value of a well-arranged and properly covered Mixture has, as already mentioned. been long recognised. It lends to the whole organ energy and decision, to the lower tones distinctness, and to the Great organ a silver-like brilliancy, Among the old organ-builders, Gottfried Silbermann (d. 1753, at Dresden) was principally successful in employing this stop, and obtaining for it due recognition. His organs in the Catholic Chapel Royal,[1] in the Frauenkirche, Dresden; Freiberg, Saxony; Anliek; Rötha, are still much admired.

In modern organs one frequently meets with names such as Silbermann Principal, Silbermann Gedackt, etc.—a proof that a just recognition of the interesting voicings of this great master has been lately awakened.

Zamminer writes: "There seems to be a disinclination to dispense with the sharp incisiveness which the clear, shrill Mixture pipes add to the bulk of the sounding organ, and to which they stand in the same relation as spice does to food." I have to thank this same scholar for the correct estimation of theory and practice, with regard to the stop, with which I headed this paragraph.

The material for Mixture stops is chiefly spotted metal, an alloy of tin and lead (see GAMBA), or "metal," as this compound is called in German organ-building parlance (see also REGISTRATION). Zinc is also used. For Echo Mixture see HARMONIA ÆTHEREA.

Montre (from the Latin *monstrare*, to show). The name given, in French organs, to the stop which, in German organs, is called Principal, and whose pipes are placed "on show," in the front part of the organ.

[1] Concerning David Schubert, Silbermann's collaborator, and his share in the building of this organ, see *Monatshefte für Musikgeschichte*, 22nd year, No. 3. The organ scholars Schweitze and Rupp have lately drawn special attention to Silbermann.

I have found the name Montre in the celebrated Moser organ at Fribourg. In the Geneva Cathedral organ I have seen, on the same manual, a Principal 16′, a Montre 8′, and a Prestant 4′. (See OCTAVE.)

Motor. See CALCANT.

Multiplex Registers. See TRANSMISSIONS.

Musette. See CHALUMEAU.

N

Nachthorn (*Fr.*, Cor de nuit; *lit.*, "night-horn"; *Dutch*, Nachthoorn). As a rule, a wide-scaled stop, of horn-like quality, which is nowadays becoming more widely used. (It is found as a 4′ stop in Breslau Cathedral, in the Berlin Garnisonskirche, and in the Albert Hall at Sheffield.) It is sometimes found as an 8′ manual stop (*e.g.* in Cavaillé-Coll's organ in the Palais de l'Industrie at Amsterdam) as well as 4′; exceptionally also as 2′, as in the Benedictine Convent at Weingarten and in the Gnadenkirche at Hirschberg.

In the celebrated Haarlem organ (see also PRESTANT), which, as is well known, has the honour of having been played by Handel, I found a strikingly characteristic 2′ Nachthorn on the manual; and in an Amsterdam organ the same stop figures on the pedal. In Groningen (also in Holland) a Nachthorn 4′ and 2′ figures in the same instrument; the use of this stop is especially frequent in the Netherlands, partly under the name of Cor de nuit, and as such found on the 2nd manual of the organ at Verviers (Link Bros.). Cavaillé-Coll has placed a Cor de nuit 8′ in the organs in the Madrid and Moscow Conservatoires, as well as at Neuilly, Amsterdam, and in Trocadero (Paris).

In the organ in St Jacob's, Hamburg, built by Schnittker in 1688, I found an 8′ Cor de nuit on the pedal, of quite original and beautiful effect when combined with the Subbass 16′. J. S. Bach played this instrument in 1723.

The organ in St Michael's, Hamburg, possesses a Nachthorn 8′ on the 2nd manual and a Nachthorn 16′ on the 4th manual — both enclosed; also the 2nd manual of the organ in Christ Church, Mannheim. Prætorius already mentions in his *Syntagma* (1615) the Nachthorn among the stops of the organ, and remarks that the Dutch constructed it as a Hohlflöte.

Nasard. See NASSAT.

Nassat. As a rule a Quint stop, $5\frac{1}{3}'$, $2\frac{2}{3}'$, $1\frac{1}{3}'$, frequently met with in fairly large organs. A flue stop with stopped pipes; also found of $10\frac{2}{3}'$ under the name of Grossnassat. In combination with the Principal 16′, the Grossnassat produces the effect of a 32′ pipe (see QUINT). As such I have seen it, for instance, in a few large organs by Haas, Schlag & Son, as well as in certain organs in Holland, *e.g.* in St Jacob's Church, The Hague.

Normalstimmung. See OCTAVE.

O

Oberpedal. See HOHLFLÖTE.

Obertöne (Overtones). See FLÛTE HARMONIQUE, GEIGENPRINCIPAL, KLANGFARBE, MIXTURE, OCTAVE, and QUINT.

Oboe (*Fr.*, Hautbois; see also BASSOON). A very frequent 8′ reed stop on the manuals, beating as well as free (see also PHYSHARMONICA). It represents (although unfortunately not always) the wind instrument of the same name, and is accordingly called in some organs Orchestral Oboe; thus, on the 3rd manual of the organs in the Kreuzkirche, Dresden, in Westminster Abbey, in Queen's Hall, and Natal. Often the lower octaves of the Oboe are continued by the Bassoon (*q.v.*). In the St François organ at Lausanne, and at Glarus, the Oboe is arranged as a free reed in a separate swell-box. A rarer kind of Oboe, of 4′ tone, is placed in the cathedrals at Ulm and Riga; also an Octave-Oboe in the Sydney Town Hall organ. If built by a master, the two stops Oboe and Clarinet (*q.v.*) make splendid solo stops, and are an ornament to any organ.

When it is possible to keep them in tune, I do not like to find any organ without Oboe, Clarinet, or Cor Anglais, even if it have but twenty stops. (See also REED STOPS.)

If one is out of reach of the organ-builder, and the organist is unable to tune the organ himself, I am of the opinion, with several colleagues, that reed stops should be replaced by characteristic flue stops of the Gamba family (see VOIX CÉLESTE). Friedr. Weigle has placed on the Echo manual of the Leutkirche organ a Labial Oboe, composed of a Viola 8′ and a Quintatön 8′. This Oboe keeps in tune like any ordinary flue stop. A similar Labial Oboe is found in the recently restored Elisabethkirche at Breslau (Schlag). (See also SONARPFEIFE.)

As an example of a fair-sized organ possessing only flue stops, I would mention here the organ in St Mark's, Munich, which, among its thirty stops, does not number a single reed, and yet is admirably effective. I have had occasion to examine this instrument in the company of its ingenious builder, Heinmeyer, of Oettingen.

A very agreeable effect may be obtained by combining the Oboe with Vienna Flute 8′ and Flauto Traverso 4′, or with Lieblich-Gedackt 16′ and 8′ and Gemshorn 4′, particularly where these stops are enclosed in a swell-box. An able organist will also produce very interesting tonal effects by blending a full, yet mellow Oboe and a Viola of good "biting" quality; but both must be enclosed. Finally, I can recommend the combination, by coupling, of the swell Oboe with the Flauto Dolce or Bourdon of the 1st manual, using the Subbass and the Harmonicabass for the pedal. See articles CLARINET and MELODIC COUPLER for useful hints for emphasising a melody and for registering by means of a fine flute, etc., borrowed from another manual (the swell being, of course, always employed). Clarinet and Oboe are, as a rule, available for the same combinations. Repeated experiments have led me to the conclusion that the Oboe must always be enclosed in a good swell-box. Not to do so means nearly always discounting the value of this stop by one-half.

Octave. This stop is found in every organ, without exception. Its character, intonation, and scale are based upon those of the Diapasons. The first Octave is half the length of the largest Diapason, the second Octave is half the length of the preceding one, and so on.[1] To a Principal 16′, then, correspond the Octaves 8′, 4′, 2′; more rarely 1′. The last two are often called Super-Octaves; thus, in the Riga organ. A 16′ Octave built of wood has been placed by the

---

[1] These proportions are not, it is true, mathematically exact (see Melde, *Akustik*, p. 277); nevertheless, they designate the proportions in use in organ-building.

side of a 16' metal Principal in St Michael's, Hamburg. Similarly, to a Principal Bass 16' on the pedal corresponds an Octave Bass 8', and where possible, in large organs, a 4' Octave (in order to perform, for instance, certain Bach trios with the *Canto Fermo* in the pedal).

The stops of the Octave whose pipes are placed in the front of the organ are sometimes called "prestants" (from the Latin *præstare*, to stand in front). Similarly, the stops of the Principal (= *Eng.*, Diapasons) are called "montres" (from the Latin *monstrare*, to show). The Octaves serve to reinforce the first harmonic, and thus lend to the longer and deeper principal pipes more precision and clearness. It is above all in small organs, not provided with mixtures, that the Octaves, with their clear and penetrating timbre, become indispensable.

However small the means, every organ of any importance ought to possess an Octave 2' (*Eng.*, Fifteenth; *Fr.*, Doublette), so useful for sustaining the Mixture (*q.v.*), although the latter, as we have seen, already includes it (see also FLAUTINO). The 4' Octave on the Great is one of the most important of all organ stops, and is rightly termed in England the 4' Principal (see DIAPASON), which it in reality is. This stop is generally used as the starting-point in tuning the organ (see TEMPERATUR). An alteration in the cycle of fifths must be made in such a manner that the twelfth fifth becomes identical with the foundation-tone or with one of its octaves; which result is obtained by tuning each fifth a trifle flat. By these slight deviations from perfect attunement, beats (or sound-pulsations) are created, and hence the term described in German as "temperament with equal beats," commonly known as "equal temperament." The fifth is first correctly attuned, and then flattened till it gives a slow pulsation. (See Töpfer, vol. i. pp. 827 *et seq.*, on Temperament and Heinrich Scheibler's mathematical tuning according to differences of vibration.)

By presupposing the Paris pitch, adopted by the conference for deciding pitch, held at Vienna, the a', which is mentioned in every organ contract, makes 870 vibrations per second at 12° Réaumur (15° Celsius = 59° Fahrenheit). Compare Blaserna's *Sound*, p. 87. By taking as basis C (the so-called physicists' C, suggested by Sauveur, adopted later on by Chladni), of 512 simple or (French) half-vibrations (explanation follows) to which a tuning fork, a', of $853\frac{1}{3}$ vibrations would correspond, the following numerical proportions, derived from the multiples of 2, are obtained:—32' C with 32; 16' C with 64; 8' C with 128; 4' C with 256; 2' C with 512; and, lastly, $\frac{1}{16}$ c, the highest c on the organ, having 16,000 half-vibrations per second (*e.g.* Riga). Compare Du Hamel's *Organ-builder*, vol. iii. p. 137.

I agree entirely with the opinion expressed by the Organ Committee of the Apostelkirche at Cologne, to the effect that an organ tuned in the winter should be slightly under normal pitch, and that A should attain 870 vibrations only in a mean temperature. (See article REED STOPS concerning the influence of temperature on organ-tuning.) This is the proper place to mention the very interesting way in which one has succeeded by means of the Double Siren (invented by Seebeck, improved upon by Cagniard de la Tour and Dove, and in its present form constructed by the great physiologist and physicist, Helmholtz) in determining with mathematical exactness the number of vibrations per second of a string, an organ-pipe, or the human voice. Long before there was anything known of vibrations and their calculations, Pythagoras (580–500 B.C.) had discovered that, if you divide a string by a bridge in such a way that the two parts produce consonances, they must be divided in the proportion of 1 : 6. If the string be divided so that two-thirds of the string remain on the right and one-third on the left, this proportion of length—1 : 2 —gives the interval of an octave; just as the proportion 2 : 3 gives the fifth, 3 : 4 the fourth, 4 : 5 the major third, and 5 : 6 the minor third. The proportions of the inversions are obtained by doubling the smaller figure of the original interval. (See also footnote in article KLANGFARBE.)

It was not until much later that it was discovered (Mersenne), from the laws regulating the movements of strings, that the simple proportions of length in strings apply in an equal manner to the number of vibrations of tones—therefore to the interval of tone on all musical instruments, and also to that immediately under our notice, viz., the organ. I have mentioned by way of example the simple relative vibrational numbers of the various octaves founded on C. Excellent illustrations, furnished with correspondingly clear explanatory text, of Helmholtz's Double Siren, to which we owe such exceedingly important results in physical acoustics, are found in Helmholtz's *Sensations of Tone*, part ii., chap. viii. p. 242 ; Tyndall's *Lectures on Sound*, ii. p. 91; Blaserna's *Theory of Sounds*, p. 120. See also Melde's *Acoustics*, § 94, for what concerns reed stops and sirens.

In illustration of the above-mentioned vibrational numbers—for instance, that of 870 for a'—I must add that, according to Tyndall, English and German physicists call a vibration a *complete* oscillation of the vibrating body, the wave of which bends the drum of the ear first inwardly and then outwardly. French physicists, on the other hand, call a vibration a backward or a forward motion of the vibrating body *in one direction only*. We have therefore to distinguish between whole vibrations and half vibrations ; and as the Paris pitch (adopted by the International Conference at Vienna) goes by the latter, I have given the numbers accordingly. The a', for instance, mentioned as having 870 French vibrations, would have 435 complete German vibrations ; the 32' C would have 32 French vibrations, but only 16 complete German ones. See also SUBBASS.

Octave Bass. An 8′ pedal stop, generally fairly powerful, and corresponding to the Bass Principal 16′. See also Bass Flute, at the close of article FLUTE.

Octave Coupler (*Ger.*, Octavcoppel; *Fr.*, Accouplement Octaviant). This stop, found, for instance, in St Peter's, Hamburg, adds to the notes played by the organist the octave above. I have often found this stop in Italian organs under the Latin designation of "Tertia Manu," *lit.*, "with a third hand." The learned Fr. Columban, abbot of the convent of Einsiedeln, designed in 1885 a coupler uniting a stop on the 1st manual with one of an upper manual, the latter speaking an octave lower. By this means, for instance, to a Flute 8′ on the 1st manual may be coupled an Æoline 8′, a Salicional 8′, a Viola 8′, etc., of an upper manual, which thus acquires a 16′ tone; or, an 8′ string-toned stop on the 1st manual may be similarly coloured by a flute stop on an upper manual. This coupler allows some interesting combinations.

The construction of the manual super- and suboctave couplers has greatly developed of late, and has justly attracted general attention. Charming Æolian Harp effects are obtained, for instance, by drawing a delicate Æoline on the swell and playing on the 1st manual with super- and sub-octave couplers drawn, employing solemn chords with the occasional aid of the swell pedal. This harmony may be slightly strengthened by the addition of the Voix céleste, allotting the melody or a judicious flute-like embroidery to a Fernflöte on the 3rd or 4th manual.

One should try to interpret certain Wagner and Reger passages with this or similar combinations, whereby the gradual employment of the Rollschweller, backwards and forwards, renders excellent service to the player in the matter of dynamic effects.

Offenflöte. See FLUTE.

Open Diapason. The English designation for the German Principal 8'.

Ophicleide 8'. This name, which at first glance appears somewhat far-fetched, is simply derived from the orchestral instrument serpent (Greek ὄφις, the snake; hence the name); in France the name Ophicleide is still employed. It is a reed stop, frequently found on the Great as well as on the swell in large new organs (*e.g.* Riga, Laeken, Boston, Helsingfors), and is intoned like a Clarinet, and its strength is proportionate to the manual on which it is found. I have found in the organ in Notre-Dame, at Antwerp (Pierre Schyven), a very effective Ophicleide 16'. I would single out this organ as a specimen of the admirable workmanship of Belgian organ-builders, both from the point of view of size and of voicing.

Sometimes one meets with Ophicleide 16′ as pedal stops; thus, in Canterbury Cathedral and in the organ at Garden City, by Roosevelt, of New York.

Orchestral Clarinet, Flute, Oboe, and Violin, see respective articles.

P

Pedalauslösung (Pedal-release), automatic. See below.

Pedalcollectiven (*Ger.*; *Fr.*, Tirasses collectives). Collective pedals. It often happens that, in playing the full organ, the organist wishes to change suddenly to a feebler manual. But his "Tutti" pedal can then be employed only for the Great. One therefore finds in fairly large organs as many pedal buttons as there are manuals. At the moment of leaving the Great manual, the organist has only to press the button corresponding in strength to the manual which he desires to employ, and he can then continue to use the pedals without being in any way prevented from returning to the original manual when he wishes it. Supposing that the organist wishes to change suddenly from a "Tutti" to a feeble Echo manual, say, the 4th; he simply presses button No. 4, and his pedal will be reduced to a Harmonicabass or an Echobass.

Among others, Heinrich Schiffner, the excellent organ-builder of Prague, has placed a remarkable kind of automatic pedal-release in the Zwickau organ. It consists in this, that for the 2nd, 3rd, or 4th manual the degree of power in the pedal regulates itself without any outside influence, and this immediately on pressing down one key of the 2nd, etc., manual. The question of an automatic pedal-release has stimulated many organ-builders to practical experiments and improvements. The automatic pedal-release can, besides, be fixed subsequently, assuming, of course, that the console is constructed purely pneumatically, and that the tubular-pneumatic action works by means of released air-pressure. The switch should act dynamically to correspond to the last manual played until the key of another manual is pressed down. There are now, besides, convenient releasing contrivances made for the switch. In modern pneumatic organs this indispensable arrangement is generally in use.

Philomela ("Nightingale"). A kind of Concert Flute, open, with double lips, of delicate and pleasing intonation, appearing often in organs built by Hook & Hastings, among others—*e.g.* at Cincinnati. This stop is also found as 8′ in the Passau Cathedral organ, and in that of St Andrew's (Mauraches).

Physharmonica. A very soft 8′ free reed stop, in which the metal tongue, instead of striking on the edge of the groove, vibrates freely within it (see also CLARINET). It is ordinarily enclosed in a special box, and has no real tube. A Physharmonica placed in an independent swell-box often produces charming effects, *e.g.* as an 8′ stop in the Berne Cathedral (Haas-Goll); as 16′ and 8′ in Brunswick Cathedral (Furtwängler & Hammer)—frequently mentioned in this book; and in the Freiburg (Mooser) and Lausanne (Kuhn) Cathedrals, where it has been built with sound-receivers and is of charming effect; also, as 16′, in the Marienkirche at Lübeck (Schulze). (See REED STOPS.)

In the Convent organ at Einsiedeln I have found, under the designation Vox Humana—evidently a mistake,—a fine Physharmonica provided with bells. In the Magdeburg Cathedral organ I have found a Harmonium 8′, a stop identical with the Physharmonica.

A charmingly effective combination may be obtained by the use of a good Flauto Traverso 4′, Lieblich-Gedackt 8′ and 16′, together with a Physharmonica, provided all these stops are enclosed. (See REGISTRATION.)

Piccolo. See FLAUTO PICCOLO.

Piffaro, a bright two-rank flute 4′ and 2′, rarely met with. I have found it in the Convent organ at Einsiedeln, made up of a Gedackt 4′ and an open 4′

stop. A fine Piffaro 8′ is found in St Peter's, Berlin (Buchholz).

Pneumatic Lever. The pneumatic lever, that is, a lever set in motion by air, is a mechanical mediator between the pressure on the keys and the resistance of the trackers and pallets. In a box filled with air and hermetically closed, there are as many little bellows connected with the trackers as there are keys on the manual, and the finger has only to apply sufficient pressure to raise a little valve. Particulars of this invention of the Englishman Barker, which considerably facilitates playing, even with couplers, will be found in Töpfer, vol. i. pp. 542 *et seq.*, and in Richter, ch. xiv. Latterly, pneumatic action has been successfully applied to draw-knobs, couplers, transmissions, etc.; and in modern organs trackers have almost disappeared.

That mechanical action has here and there its adherents, even in Germany, is shown by a footnote by Rupp in the *Z. f. I.*, according to which the excellent firm of Haerpper & Dalstein, of Bolchen, has quite lately received an order to build two tracker organs. I have had the opportunity of examining, with reference to its tonal qualities, and under the personal guidance of the genial Strassburg expert, Dr Albert Schweitzer, an organ built by the above-named masters. Among other well-voiced stops, some exquisitely graceful Gedackts attracted my attention, the prompt speech and effect of which are due in no small measure to the artistically judicious reduction of the air-pressure.

I might mention here many other interesting modern inventions concerning the thoroughly perfected tubular-pneumatic action, the rôle of electricity in organ-building (see ELECTRO-PNEUMATIC), free membranes, the employment of mercury, platinum, silver, etc., the combined use of tubular-pneumatic with Kegellade sound-boards, high-pressure stops, etc., Biehle's theory, Silbermann's scales, etc., and compare these innovations with the old systems. But after careful thought and counselling with very authoritative colleagues, I have decided to keep myself within the limits of a more exclusively musical horizon, and to content myself—in accordance with the title of my book—with treating of the character of the different stops of the organ and their combinations, and of the acoustic phenomena which they present. I leave to organists and organ-builders —as outlined in my preface—the task of experimenting upon the practical value of this or that system or invention. This applies especially to the numerous inventions in the direction of multiplex registers, of twin-manuals, the manifold uses to which the same stop may be put, and the complicated possibilities by the further use of transmission. All these things are widely outside the scope of "Klangfarbe," and are fully discussed in technical publications.

The measuring of time employed by air-currents in pneumatic tubes, based upon mathematically correct experiments on the part of Johannes Biehle, Edmund Ehrenhofer, and Friedrich Drexler with the help of electricity, are of importance in organ-building, and especially with regard to pneumatics. The practical results of these recent experiments, which recall the earlier researches of the famous Töpfer, have already been discussed in various technical reviews. But in a book which is concerned only with "Klangtints" and their combinations, I can do no more than just point out these new discoveries in the realm of organ-pneumatics.

Pneumatic Pistons (or buttons) (*Ger.*, Pneumatische Druckknöpfe; *Fr.*, Boutons pneumatiques) are to be found almost everywhere, affixed above, below, or at the sides of the respective manuals, on the moulding of the keyboard. Their use affords a graduated registration without affecting the stops prepared by the organist.

In the Riga Cathedral organ (124 stops), where the organist has quite enough to do with hands and feet, I found such a simple method of registering most convenient. Pistons and tilting-tablets are also affixed to advantage in smaller organs.

In the place of the older draw-knobs, pistons or tablets are now frequently used. These respond to a slight pressure of the finger, and thus ensure quick changes of stops. Organ-builders display much ingenuity in the arrangements of their consoles (*q.v.*). One notices innovations in nearly every new organ.

Mention should also be made here of the important endeavours which have been made at the well-known Vienna Congress for the standardisation of organ-building. I am convinced that organ-builders will be able to avail themselves advantageously of many hints. The numerous artists among them, each in his special capacity, will again know, from the results attained, how to draw logical conclusions from the Congress for the advancement and glory of the art of organ-building. I would draw special attention to the excellent essays and discussions at the Vienna Congress, which have appeared in the best professional journals, from the competent pens of Arthur Egidis, Edm. Ehrenhofer, Max Allihn, Dr. Hainisch, Schnorr von Carolsfeld, Dr. Schweitzer, Emil Rupp, and other authorities.

Mention must also be made here of the so-called stop keyboard affixed to the choir organ in Freiburg Cathedral, answering the purpose of draw-knobs, and which is also affixed above the manual as a special keyboard or as a continuation of the keyboard. (See also PROLONGEMENT.) Here I would again call the reader's attention to the advice given by Hermann Ley, organist of Lübeck Cathedral, at the close of his excellent essay on "Organs, Organ-playing, and Organ-building," published in the *Z. f. I.*

Easily accessible (see CRESCENDO) Rollschweller, excellently adapted in the centre above the pedalboard, *e.g.* in Berlin Cathedral and at Esslingen; pistons; uniformity in keyboard measurements, in depth of keys, in the distance from keyboard to pedal (*vide* Prussian Ministerial Decree of February 5, 1904, as the result of a recommendation of the German Organ-builders' Society); in the proximity of the keyboards; the avoidance of any plan which may render manipulation more difficult, etc.,—are all greatly to be desired in large organs.

I have already mentioned elsewhere that collective registers for bringing on combinations by means of pedals as well as by pistons, should be lettered.

Highly interesting is also the essay on *Aids to Playing*, by Max Allihn, and the treatise on *Modern Art of Organ-building*, published by the Bros. Rieger, organ-builders in Jägerndorf, on the occasion of the completion of their op. No. 1000, etc.

Portunalflöte (Portunal flute). An 8' and 4' manual flute stop, ordinarily of wood, generally open, more rarely stopped. Its pipes, like those of the Dolce, are constructed slightly widening at the top. This stop is somewhat rare. Allihn derives this word from Bordun. I have found, in the excellent organ in St John's Church, Leipzig (Roever), a very fine Portunalflöte 8' on the 3rd manual—half Gemshorn and half Flute in character. This same stop is found under the name Portunal 8′ at Freiburg (Schlag), in St Michael's, Hamburg (Walcker), etc.

Posaune (Trombone). A beating reed stop found in nearly all large organs, and which should imitate its orchestral prototype. More rarely the Trombone is a free reed stop; thus, in the Lutherkirche at Frankfurt a. M., and in an organ at Pilsen, built by Brauner. After the Tuba Mirabilis (*q.v.*), the Trombone is the most powerful stop of the organ. On this account it is necessary, therefore, that it be supported by an adequate number of full and sonorous stops, in order that it shall not predominate.

In medium-sized organs, the Trombone is advantageously replaced by the Bombarde, which is somewhat softer. The Trombone is constructed generally as a 16′ stop, sometimes as 32′, *e.g.* the Trombone of the organ at Wesel, built by Sauer.

In the 128-stop organ in the Town Hall, Sydney, built by William Hill, of London, there is a Contra-trombone 64′ on the pedal. From the point of view of acoustics this is a somewhat risky experiment. It goes without saying that this gigantic stop can only be employed with the full organ, and that it must be supported by an adequate number of 32′ and 16′ stops.

Helmholtz, who, from the first, took a lively interest in this little work, wrote to me saying that he doubted very much whether a 64′-stop could be of real use. In his monumental work, *Die Lehre von den*

Tonempfindungen, the great physicist estimates that the Subcontra A, yielding twenty-eight vibrations per second (French system), is the gravest sound which the human ear can perceive. This assertion has recently been contested, and it has been contended that the limit of perceptible sounds is found an octave and a half lower, or thereabouts. (See *Urania*, below.)

Dr von Schack, of Rotterdam, has made some experiments in order to elucidate this point. He fixed in a vice and caused to vibrate a steel spring a millimetre in thickness and 26 millimetres in width, provided with a plate 8 centimetres wide on its upper edge. As one pushes down this plate deeper tones are obtained. These experiments have proved that Helmholtz was right. The Subcontra A was, in effect, the deepest tone perceptible. The G immediately below was only occasionally perceptible, and then only under particularly favourable circumstances. In the case of lower notes the foundation-tone was absolutely lost, only the upper tones being audible. Thus, when the plate was fixed at Subcontra D♯ one heard only the octave and the twelfth above. The presence of the foundation-tone was signalled only by the vibration of the air, so that one could, so to speak, *see* this sound, but could no longer *hear* it. (With reference to these acoustical phenomena, see SUBBASS.) The same result has been arrived at by experimenting with immense stopped pipes, 10 metres long. In this case also the Subcontra A was heard, but already more feebly than the B♭. The G was heard only occasionally, and the F♯ not at all.

The upward limit of sounds perceptible to the human ear is less definitely fixed. Generally speaking, it may be said that the sharpest sound we can perceive is the *c* of the ninth octave, yielding 16,896 vibrations per second. The scale of sounds perceptible to our ears embraces, therefore, nearly ten octaves. (See *Urania*, 52nd year, p. 98.)

The body of the Trombone has the shape of a square inverted pyramid, and is generally constructed of wood. A tin body would perhaps render the tone more brilliant and expressive. (See also REED STOPS.)

Prestant (or Prästant). In the very interesting organ in St Bavo's, Haarlem (Bazuin) (played upon by Handel) I found a 32′ open Prestant on the pedal, which, accompanied by 32′ and 16′ Bass Trombones, is of magnificent effect. I do not wish to forego the opportunity of thanking here M. Ezermann, the genial Haarlem organist, who invited me to examine his superb instrument, and from whom I have received much cordial encouragement in the production of this work. This particular organ only lacks the recently discovered facilities which the pneumatic system offers. The front of this magnificent instrument is not only the finest I know of in Holland, but, I believe, also one of the finest extant anywhere. And I do not stand alone in my opinion. The *Z. f. I.* (23rd year,

No. 3) also mentions this front and reproduces an excellent drawing of it. This same journal also reproduces the front of the new organ in Seville Cathedral. See also NACHTHORN.

Principal (fig. 8) (*Fr.*, Montre, *q.v.*; *Eng.*, Diapason) is the most important flue stop of the organ. It is found without exception in every organ, and forms the basis of the harmony. Its pipes are constructed preferably of pure tin (see GAMBA); they constitute the front of the organ (see ELECTRO-PNEUMATIC). A Principal with fine and well-polished pipes of English tin is generally recognised as one of the finest assets of the organ (see FISTULA). In organs of two or more manuals, the Principals on each manual are constructed of different scale. In a two-manual instrument, for instance, the Principal of the Great organ is of large scale (see GEIGENPRINCIPAL).

In organs of medium or small size, the Principal is always 8'—that is to say, the longest pipe of this stop measures about 8'. For the sake of symmetry, longer pipes are sometimes

FIG. 8.—Principal. Pitch coincides with that of the same length Gamba (fig. 5), which is of slender scale in order to obtain the Gamba string-tone.

placed in the front, but they are cut at the back, so that the sounding-tube shall be of the required length. I have found, in a recent examination of organs, the longest pipes of the Principal replaced, owing to lack of space, by a Gedackt 8′, accompanied by a soft Octave 4′, and this without any great disadvantage. But, wherever possible, I undoubtedly prefer pipes of pure English tin: and this applies also to the Gamba and the Violoncello. Large organs often have two Principals on the Great manual— a 16′ and an 8′. In the organ in St Denis, Cavaillé-Coll has placed a Principal 32′ on the 2nd manual —a rare occurrence. (By "2nd manual" the Great manual is here meant; and this is the case, for instance, with organs in Paris, Vienna, Fribourg, Geneva, and elsewhere; also with English and American organs.—TR.) In the Kaiser Wilhelm Gedächtniskirche, Berlin (Sauer), I have found no less than nine Principals, all voiced by a master-hand; and in the Cathedral of the same city, the new organ in which has also been built by Sauer, the 1st manual possesses, in addition to a Principal 16′, a Majorbass 16′. In St Michael's, Hamburg, a Metallprinzipal 8′ has been placed side by side with a Principal Major. Even medium-sized organs have generally a Principal 16′ on the pedal (see also CONTRABASS). Another rarity might here be noticed: in the island of Jersey, in a three-manual organ built by Robson, I have found, under the name of Grand Open Pedal, an Open

Principal 16′ as the only pedal stop for the three manuals; it is a stop of extraordinarily large scale (see Töpfer, part i. p. 126), and of a power recalling the corresponding pedal stop found in St Lawrence's, St Gallen. The same proportion of pedal stops is frequently found in organs by American builders. Roosevelt, of New York, for instance, in one of his organs, containing thirty-three speaking stops, has placed only three stops on the pedal, *i.e.* a Principal 16′, a Subbass 16′, and a Violoncello 8′. An attempt has been made to remedy this poverty of pedal stops by a great variety of couplers, affecting single and whole groups of stops.

In very large organs, a 32′ Open Principal Bass is found, generally of wood. When constructed of tin— as is the case, for instance, in the Lucerne Hofkirche and in Ulm Cathedral—the largest pipe of this stop weighs about 450 kilos; its diameter is 18 inches, and its circumference about 5 feet. According to Töpfer (part ii. p. 200), a pipe of these dimensions requires 1536 cubic inches of wind per second, while c^1—middle C—needs only 99·4, and c^5 but 6·4. A Principalbass 32′, valuable in a double sense, has been built entirely of 15½-oz. tin by Walcker for the front of the gigantic organ in St Michael's, Hamburg. This stop weighs about 4250 kilos. This grand five-manual instrument, with its 163 speaking stops, has been made possible through the munificence of a generous patron, whose memory will be always cherished in

PRINCIPAL

this connection. I have had permission to examine the factory and the arrangements made for the reception of this unique organ. The specification of the instrument—providing for a number of stops unattained by any other instrument up to the present (and some of which I had occasion to inspect in the Ludwigsburg factory)—is due, in addition to the builder, to an artistic committee and to the celebrated Dresden organist, Prof. Sittard.

The organists whom I had the pleasure of meeting on the occasion of my late sojourn in Hamburg had the kindness to personally demonstrate their various and, for the most part, interesting organs.

The 32′ Open wood Principal Bass (in some organs erroneously described as Subbass) is already coming into general use in all countries.

I have already referred elsewhere to the imposing effect produced by a 32′ stop in a crescendo. The weight of the Contra C pipe of such a gigantic stop is about 800 kilos, and its walls have a thickness of $2\frac{1}{2}$ inches, so as to offer a sufficient resistance to the column of air; for the walls of pipes are not absolutely immobile: one can perfectly well feel them vibrating at the same time as the column of air. In order that powerful vibrations may result (Zamminer) the air must be surrounded by resisting walls; if these are loose and yielding, the vibratory movement is transmitted to the surrounding air, and the force of the sound-wave is lost before it has attained the upper orifice of the tube. (See also REGISTRATION, OCTAVE, DIAPASON, and FLUE STOPS.)

Principal Amabile. A small Principal of soft intonation, found, for instance, on the 3rd manual of the organ at Apolda (Sauer).

Principalbass. See PRINCIPAL.

Principalflöte 8'. A stop of bright, agreeable, flute-like quality, advantageously placed on the 2nd manual of some organs, *i.e.* Hochdorf (Lucerne), and blending nicely with Salicional, Viola, or Æoline. Sauer, in his organ in the Johanniskirche at Dorpat, employs the designation Principalflöte 8'.

Principal major. See PRINCIPAL.

Probezinn. See GAMBA.

Progressio is a non-repeating (*i.e.* with no "breaks") stop, more closely described under MIXTURES.

Progressiv-Harmonica. See HARMONICA.

Prolongement. There are two kinds:—(1) The Combinations-prolongement. This is a button which permits the organist to prepare at will, whilst he is playing, a new combination, which does not become effective until the button in question is pressed. This appliance is to be found, for instance, in the large organ built by Walcker for Riga.

(2) The Prolongement harmonique, which I have found, for instance, in an organ exhibited by Cavaillé-Coll. It is a contrivance governed by a pedal, and which permits, for instance, during a "point d'orgue," to leave the keys without their being thereby released, and thus enabling one to use one's hands in order to prepare a new combination, which latter does not become effective until the player releases the pedal in question.

Q

Querflöte. See FLAUTO TRAVERSO.

Quintadena. See QUINTATÖN.

Quintadena Bass. See QUINTATÖN.

Quintatön. A stop which, in addition to the foundation-tone, yields also, though very lightly, the quint of the upper octave, otherwise called the twelfth. Hence its Latin name of *Quintam tenens*. (See Helmholtz, p. 152.)

The Quintatön belongs to the family of Gedackts, and owes its properties to its narrow scale (see GEDACKT).

The 2nd manual of the organ at Horgen possesses a fine Quintatön 16′; and in the recently built organ in the Kaiser Wilhelm Gedächtniskirche at Berlin, I have found no less than three Quintatöns: 16′ (on the Echo manual), 8′, and 4′. In St Peter's, Leipzig, I have found a very fine Quintatön 8′ on the pedal. The Madeleine organ in Paris possesses a Quintatön 32′ (rarely found); in the organ of the Convent at Einsiedeln a Quintadena bass 8′, and in the Brunswick Cathedral organ (Furtwängler) a Quintatön bass 8′.

The Quintatön is incomparable for blending Flute and Gamba stops (see GAMBA, first paragraph). A quite original effect may be obtained by combining a fine Quintatön with a well-voiced and enclosed Voix céleste.

Zamminer (p. 265) gives the following information concerning this valuable stop:—" The bore of a Quintatön should be large for an open pipe and narrow for a stopped pipe; and it is owing to this that this stop yields the fifth of the upper octave. This effect is intensified if the mouth is cut very low and the wind-pressure is augmented."

Quintbass. See QUINT.

Quinte (Quint). A very well-known accessory or mutation stop, reinforcing the second harmonic. Its pipes are sometimes open, of the same scale and power as those of the Principal, and sometimes conical, in which case it takes the name of Gemshorn Quint (Quinte de chamois), Spitzquint (Quinte à fuseau), or Nassatquint (Quinte de Nasard). It is found both as a manual and a pedal stop.

The dimensions of the Quint are $10\frac{2}{3}'$ ($=\frac{32}{3}'$), $5\frac{1}{3}'$, $2\frac{2}{3}'$, and $1\frac{1}{3}'$, according to the dimensions of the Principal to which it corresponds. Thus, for a Principal 16', the Quint should be, from the point of view of acoustics, $10\frac{2}{3}'$; for a Principal 8', $5\frac{1}{3}'$; for an Octave 4', $2\frac{2}{3}'$; for an Octave 2', $1\frac{1}{3}'$. But in practice a Quint $10\frac{2}{3}'$ is made to correspond to a Bass Principal 32', and so on. That is to say, the scale of the Quint is always a third less than that of its Principal, and this because the Quint is by nature the third harmonic of its foundation-tone (Eberle).

Mention must be made here of the discovery of resultant tones by Sorge, and to which Tartini gave their name; their origin was explained by Helmholtz. The Abbé Vogler, Court Kapellmeister (d. 1814, at Darmstadt), utilised this discovery: by sounding simultaneously a Quint $10\frac{2}{3}'$ and a Principal 16', a 32' tone is obtained—for instance, in the organ in the Convent at Einsiedeln; from the union of a Principal 8' and a Quint $5\frac{1}{3}'$ a 16' tone results. One can easily see how this makes for economy. (See also PRINCIPAL.)

The application of this discovery to the formation of 32' tone may be seen in the organ at Glarus (Walcker), in the Tonhalle at Zürich (Kuhn), in the Temple-du-Bas at Neuchâtel, in the Garnisonskirche at Ulm (Link), and (for the 32′ acoustic from low A downwards) in the Apostelkirche at Cologne (Goll). I have often recommended this way of getting out of a difficulty in the case of churches where the necessary height was wanting. Nevertheless, I am of the opinion, with others, that, in order to accompany certain particularly expressive passages on the 3rd and 4th manuals, a true 32′ is needed, the above-mentioned resultant 32′—which might be styled *acoustic*—being liable to a slight " quint," which is harmful to the effect of certain soft passages. The 32′ "acoustic" can be employed for the deeper tones.

An original effect may be obtained by supporting an Echo Trumpet placed in the swell by a softly voiced 32′. (See a similar combination at the close of the article TRUMPET.)

As I have just mentioned the matter of economy in materials, it seems interesting to mention here the so-called "Zwei-ton" ("two-tone") system employed by the Bros. Rieger at Jägerndorf. These builders construct their pipes—especially the large pedal pipes—in such a manner that each can yield two tones; for instance, C can yield at will C or C♯. I am told that this system works noiselessly and without fear of derangement. It is unnecessary to say that, in addition, it economises space. Its application is also to be found at Aussig, Rome, Cracow, Ratibor,

Warsaw, Vienna, and elsewhere. The Bass Quint $10\tfrac{2}{3}'$ may also be employed in soft passages, viz. in Guilmant's " Pastorale," in Saint-Saëns' " Symphony with Organ " (Luz). Mention must also be made here of the interesting application of acoustic stops made by Walcker in the Vienna Votivkirche. He has combined a Principal bass 16', an Octave 8', and an Octave bass 4' together with a Quint bass $10\tfrac{2}{3}'$ and a Tierce bass $6\tfrac{2}{5}'$ in order to produce a Grand Bourdon 32'. Gottschalg wrote: " The blending of these five pedal stops, which might be looked upon as a gigantic quintuple pedal Fourniture, produces a sound of great power." They are naturally placed upon a special wind-chest. Similar quintuple Grands Bourdons are found at Mühlhausen, Ulm, and Riga. For the seven-rank Gross-mixtur in St Michael's, Hamburg, see MIXTURE.

A stopped Quint, with plugs provided with a small pipe, is called a Rohrquinte (Quinte à cheminée) (see ROHRFLÖTE). I have found a Rohrquinte on the pedal of many organs in Holland—for instance, in the monumental Haarlem organ. A Rohrquinte $10\tfrac{2}{3}'$ has been placed in the pedal of the organ in St Michael's, Hamburg. The Quint, like the Mixtures, is in general used only with the full organ.

For the numerical ratios of simple intervals with the foundation-tone, see OCTAVE and KLANGFARBE.

Quintflöte. See QUINT.

R

Rauschquinte, Rauschflöte (*Fr.*, Quinte bruyante, Flûte bruyante; *rausch*, lit., loud, blustering). A stop ordinarily made up of Quint $2\frac{2}{3}'$ and Octave $2'$, that is to say, of the quint and its upper octave. These two tones together form a fourth, which gives this stop its peculiar rustling. I have found this useful stop even in small organs, where it replaces advantageously a multiple-rank mixture. In large instruments the Rauschquinte is almost indispensable and renders valuable services, even in the mezzoforte. (See also CORNETTINO.)

The Rauschquinte sometimes replaces the Fourniture in the upper manuals, and it can also be placed on the Great for strengthening purposes in place of the Octave $2'$. Such is the case in the Zürich Tonhalle and in the organ at Stein a. Rhein. The organ in St Mary's, Lübeck (Schulze), possesses two such stops: one $2\frac{2}{3}'$ (stopped), and the other $2'$ (open).

Reed Stops (*Ger.*, Zungenwerk, Zungenstimmen; *Fr.*, Jeux à anches) (fig. 9). As this term comprises a whole species of stops, in contradistinction to Flue stops, and as it occurs frequently in the course of this work, I deem it advisable to give a thorough definition of it, in accordance with technical works on the subject, and my own numerous essays and observations.

REED STOPS 125

The current of air coming from the sound-board

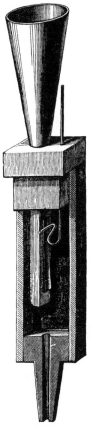

FIG. 9.—Longitudinal section of a reed pipe, with sounding cup.

FIG. 10.—Reed pipe divested of cup, and side view of tongue, l, set in motion by the current of air coming from F.

sets in vibration an elastic tongue (*i.e.* a strip of metal, fig. 10, l), which periodically intercepts the stream of air (by alternately opening and closing). Regarding the use of beech-wood for reeds, see CLARINET.

These vibrations of the tongue, or rather the intermittent impulses of the wind (see Melde's *Akustik*, p. 308), which at each vibration break through the aperture closed by the tongue, produce the tone, the height or depth of which depends upon the number of the vibrations. How very different the construction of flue pipes is from that of reed pipes is evident from the fact that in the latter the visible part of the pipe (*i.e.* the resonant tube, as in fig. 9) in no way contributes to the real production of the tone, but only serves musically to refine the sound which originates at the tongue, to impart to it the requisite tone-colour (*Klangfarbe*), and to strengthen it after the manner of a speaking-trumpet (*Sprachrohrartig*).

The height of these resonant tubes, however, is strictly limited according to the height of tone required (see TRUMPET); Haas, for instance, ruled that in blowing across the upper edges of the tube (see Tyndall, *Eight Lectures on Sound*, p. 212) this cavity should produce a tone half a note higher than the note for which the tube is intended. If one wishes to determine, for instance, whether a tube has the right length for c, the hollow of the cup, if blown in the manner above described, should give $c\sharp$.

As I have said, the pitch of the tone depends upon the number of the vibrations of the tongue, which are regulated by the tuning-wire (fig. 10, d). The scale of the tubes depends upon the pitch produced by the greater or lesser vibrations of the tongue; the lower tones naturally requiring larger and longer tubes, the higher ones smaller and shorter ones. The tongue is fastened over a metal groove or reed (fig. 10, *r*), which, when at rest, it closes, with the exception of a very fine chink all round its margin. The tongue is either allowed to vibrate freely *in* the groove (see PHYSHARMONICA), in which case it is said to be *a free reed* (Ger., *freischwingden* ; Fr., *anche libre*), or, with each vibration it strikes *against the edge* of the groove, and is then called a beating or striking reed (Ger., *aufschlagend* ; Fr., *anche battante*). In order to soften the frequently harsh tone produced by metal beating against metal, the modern art of organ-building has very cleverly resorted to fine leather covering for the edges of the grooves.

Fig. 10, *pp*, represents the air-chamber, where the groove and tongue are fixed between the wedge and the block SS. Figs. 9 and 10 represent longitudinal sections, to allow of an inspection of the cleverly arranged interior parts of this species of pipe.

In consequence of the intense influence which cold and heat exercise upon flue stops, and the difference in pitch from that of the reeds resulting therefrom, these latter frequently require tuning. I will give only one example of the extraordinary influence of temperature on sound: the velocity of sound in air at zero Centigrade (32° Fahrenheit) is 1090 feet per second; it increases about 2 feet for every degree of Celsius as the temperature rises. A cold column of air yields a deeper tone (see OCTAVE) than the same column if warmed and therefore rarefied; for, in spite of the same length of the waves, the tone in warm air is higher than in cold air because of the *quicker succession* of these waves. By heat the pitch of flue pipes is, therefore, raised considerably higher than that of reeds, which is flattened by the extension, and consequent slackening, of the tongue in the same temperature. The thermal influence on the number of vibrations of a riveted tongue (Physharmonica, Harmonium) has been proved by Zellner to be infinitesimally small.

This is a proof that, contrary to general opinion, reed stops with sounding tubes are less subject to changes of temperature, and their effect upon true pitch, than are flue stops, and that, if there is a difference of pitch between these two species of pipes, it is generally brought about by a change in the flue pipes. The trials made in various organ factories fully bear out this argument. These trials were carried out with a Trumpet and an Octave, which were first justly tuned to the pitch of a tuning-fork, and were then subjected to artificially produced changes of temperature.

For technical reasons (see FLUE PIPES), the tuning of flue pipes should remain the business of the organ-builder; the organist, therefore, in his attempts to bring his instrument back to the proper pitch, is limited to the re-tuning of the reeds only. But it is easily understood that even this operation, which is based upon a delicate handling of the tongue (*q.v.*) by the tuning-wire, should be performed only by conscientious and experienced hands. And though one may always expect conscientiousness in country organists, yet it would not be fair to look for the requisite experience. One refrains, therefore, from the inclusion of reed stops in very small country organs, and tries to replace them in a measure by the substitution of characteristic stops like the Voix céleste (*q.v.*), or by incisive and string-toned stops like the Gamba, Viola, Salicional, Geigenprincipal. (See also OBOE.) Where, however, the organist is capable of undertaking the regular tuning of the reeds, and the construction of the instrument has been entrusted to a skilled builder, it would be regrettable to omit to provide an Oboe, a Clarinet, a Trumpet, etc., solely on account of economy.

With regard to tuning, I venture to remark that I do not care to see it done by either forcing down the tuning-wire or pulling it out with a pair of pincers, in which operation the tuning-wire is so often bent or even broken; rather should this, if at all possible, be done with the aid of a properly constructed reed-knife, by which the wire can only be moved vertically up or down. It is always best at once to replace damaged wires, or such on which the knife has no proper hold for want of a notch,[1] because the knife might slip off and damage the sides of the pipes.

How important must be a moderate and æsthetically discerning choice of reeds for the flue work, is evident from the fact that no manner of construction is yet known (see, however, TROMPETTE HARMONIQUE) by which it is possible to impart to the upper notes of reeds the strong, piercing tone which, in certain registers, is peculiar to flue pipes, and by which the latter, in a measure, lose their great strength in the lower notes, where, *per contra*, the reeds begin to be more decidedly effective. Töpfer (*Orgelbaukunst*, p. 104) places this distinctly perceptible relative effect of these two species of pipes upon each other in the tenor octave.

This difference of power is most apparent in the pedal stops, which explains the important part played by the pedals in compositions for the organ. (See also Marx, *Kompositionslehre*, pt. i., bk. ii. p. 330.)

While, for instance, a 32′ Principalbass or a 32′ open Subbass develops a majestic depth and fullness which, somehow, are often only felt, the Trombone or the Tuba Mirabilis (*q.v.*) will always have a power and distinctness which, in a way, grate on the ear. Only a judicious and well-thought-out employment of both

---

[1] See Töpfer's *Atlas der Orgelbaukunst*, diagram cv., fig. 937, which represents a reed pipe with the upper end of the tuning-wire (not visible in our fig. 10), and in which this sharp notch is clearly discernible.

kinds of pipe will evidently result in a perfect combination.[1]

One might attribute to the difference in national character the fact that, whereas the Germans and the Dutch prefer to hear the peaceful tone of a flue pipe, the French incline towards the more lively character of a Trumpet, the Italians towards the peculiar mystic character of their "Ripieno" (often of 6 to 8 ranks), and the English their brilliant Diapasons and string-toned stops. I agree with my eminent colleagues that perfection in these various departments seems to become always more and more the speciality of the international art of organ-building.

The *Grundriss der musikalischen Akustik*, by the learned Dr. A. Jonquière, of Berne, contains some interesting information on the relations between reed and flue pipes. I could myself adduce many examples of the kind.

I shall not discuss here the question as to whether a reason for the comparatively frequent inclusion of expensive reeds in organs may not be found in the fact that the organ-builder demands and obtains a proportionately higher price for the sacrifice of time and labour which these stops entail.

I cannot refrain from warmly echoing the wish of

[1] I can but draw once more the reader's attention to the golden advice contained in Edm. Ehrenhofer's valuable *Taschenbuch des Orgelbaurevisors*, bottom of p. 4 and p. 251 (proportion of voices —"Stimmenverhältnis").

my late friend, Gottschalg (*Urania*, 35th year, p. 175, and 44th year, pp. 37 and 63), and of the excellent organist, the late Prof. S. de Lange (Leipzig: *Musik. Wochenblatt*, 13th year, No. 22), viz. that the conscientious and clever builder ought to be suitably recompensed, in order to enable him to keep pace with his competitors. If in every walk of life " the labourer is worthy of his hire," how much more true this is in a domain where he attains the rank of an artist! (See VOICING.)

Finally, I would quote here what my late colleague, C. L. Werner, wrote, among other things, and with much truth, in *Urania*: " Organs are sometimes built at prices for which no builder can turn out good work, unless he wants to starve." People are everywhere beginning to realise that an organ well constructed in all its component parts is a work of art, and, as such, cannot be built at a low figure. The financial question always plays an important part in such matters.

Among the numerous articles, written by experts, which have appeared on this subject, I would mention, as especially interesting, what the brothers Link, excellent organ-builders, have written under the title " Orgeldispositionen " in the *Z. f. I.*, 21st year, No. 11.

I have digressed somewhat from my subject, but I do not regret it if, by these few thoughts, I have been able to contribute, in however feeble a manner, to the progress of the noble art of organ-building.

I would also mention an interesting Italian organ-building novelty which I saw in Milan, in the shape of a working specimen of an organ with leather-pulp pipes prepared by a chemical process.

In the course of time very different materials have been employed in the construction of organ-pipes, and this has been found to be not without influence on the tone-colour ("Klangfarbe") of the stops (Prof. von Schafhäutl and Fr. Zamminer).

If, nevertheless, it is borne in mind that modern builders have succeeded, by artistic voicing, in rendering almost imperceptible the transition from metal to wood (see ÆOLINE) in certain stops; if one further considers the scientifically proved fact (see FLUE STOPS) that the body of the pipe serves only to regulate the vibrating column of air and to separate it from the outer atmosphere, one is tempted to believe that the influence of materials on the quality of sound has been exaggerated.

Melde, in his *Akustik*, p. 242, proposes divers materials for experimental purposes, such as metal, zinc, tin-plate, lead, brass, glass, wood, and pasteboard, and on p. 247 furnishes some interesting tables of the vibrational results obtained with cylindrical pasteboard tubes. Regarding experiments made with ivory pipes, see FISTULA and GAMBA.

I therefore accepted with much pleasure the kind invitation of Fr. Crespi Reghizzo, professor of physics, and inventor of that material which threatened the organ with a "paper age," to examine personally the organ *a canne di cartone* ("with pasteboard pipes") at Milan. On entering the Oratorio di Santa Cristina, the front visible in the background reminded me of the similarly painted English show-pipes already mentioned (see PRINCIPAL), save that, in this case, the grounding was leather-coloured. With the help of the organist, Giovanni Amici, and of the inventor himself, I was enabled to acquaint myself with the effects of this innovation, which had been loudly discussed by the press. As the instrument was erected by a physicist and an intelligent modellist, without the aid of a practical organ-builder, and as its sole object was to prove the usefulness of a new material for organ-pipes, I will limit myself to making the following mention of the trial.

An open cylindrical 8′ stop, compared with my tuning-fork (870 French vibrations for a), gave the exact Paris pitch. The general effect of the pasteboard pipes was surprisingly loud and bright, the Mixture (*Ripieno*) powerful, and the whole tone on the whole satisfactory.

To my ear—somewhat spoilt, perhaps—there was wanting the brilliant, metallic, and yet rounded character of the Trumpet and the incisive harmonic string-tone of a slender-scale, powerfully blown Gamba supplied with a Frein harmonique, as well as the enchanting delicacy of our Lieblich-Gedackts, Voix célestes, Salicionals, and Æoline. But perhaps these deficiencies were partly due to the fact, already mentioned, that the skilled hand of the practical voicer had taken no part in the work.

Without intending or being able to supplant English tin, spotted metal, zinc, or the wood of the fir, oak, pear, and maple, the peculiarity and sound-producing qualities of which Reghizzo by no means underrates, this new material might still, on account of its unrivalled cheapness, sooner or later assume its modest place among the existing materials.

A modest beginning towards such an amalgamation has already been made with these pasteboard pipes. In reed pipes, for instance, the air-chamber, block, and cup are of pasteboard; the groove and wedge, on the other hand, are of wood; and the tongue is a thin strip of brass, thickest where it is screwed on, and tapering into a thin blade towards the lower end. The brass tuning-wire in no way differs from that already in use. In the Gedackts and flue pipes all parts are of leather pulp, with the exception of the block (*anima*), which is of hard wood, and the stopper similar to our fig. 6.

According to Pestalozzi, Joh. Heinr. Freitag produced, as early as 1781, an organ "manufactured entirely of paper" (Schweizer, *Künstlerlexikon*).

It is evident that the most renowned organ-builders of all countries, who are frequently cited as real artists in their profession, will not leave unnoticed such a cheap and easily transportable material especially if, in the long run, it should show sufficient resistance to the influence of temperature, and stability with regard to pitch. Meanwhile, organists, organ-builders, and church authorities still maintain a prudent reserve with regard to the employment of this new material, preferring still the materials which have been successfully employed for centuries, and are incomparably superior from an æsthetic point of view, and are to-day even made to conform, according to the peculiarities of each case, to the style of the churches.

Experienced friends, whose advice has been invaluable to me from the beginning, agree that it was part of the task of this work to mention this new and deserving invention of the gifted Italian priest.

After having devoted nearly a chapter to the fortunately rare paper organs, there remains only the agreeable duty of rendering a deserved tribute to the Italian art of organ-building. Since the appearance of the Italian edition of this book (published by Ulrico Hoepli in Milan), the most important Italian organ-builders have had the kindness to keep me posted, by repeated interesting information, of their largely excellent new organs. With them also the motto " Excelsior !" seems to hold good.

Regal. A family of obsolete reed stops, of which one finds here and there isolated examples, such as the Geigenregal and the Jungfernregal.

Registerausschaltungen (Eliminating Registers). See TRUMPET.

Registerclaviatur (Stop-keys or Fitting-tablets) instead of Draw-knobs. See PISTONS.

Registerpneumatik. See PNEUMATIC.

Registerwalze. See ROLLSCHWELLER.

Registration (*Ger.*, Registermischungen). It will be understood that the modest limits of my work do not allow me to discuss at any great length the art of registration, or to reproduce a great number of specifications. Nevertheless, I have deemed it useful to give some further hints on effective registration at the close of certain articles. The new journeys and examinations of organs which I have recently undertaken have furnished me with fresh material (see Preface). It goes without saying that these remarks are not at all exhaustive of the subject, and that they are subject to modification according to the peculiarities of each organ. I believe, nevertheless, that they cannot be without interest to my esteemed colleagues, seeing that they are based upon a very varied experience. An organist of even most modest attainments will see that over and over again I have tried to show the relationship and analogy existing between stops which are otherwise distinguished from each other strictly according to their fundamental tone. I have pointed out, for instance, that the Flautino and the Flageolet must be accompanied by deeper-toned stops; that the Bombarde and the Trombone need a sufficient number of flue stops to counterbalance them; that the Mixture, the Acuta (*Scharf*), and the Cymbal can be employed only in the Tutti.

In the articles Flue Stops, Fourniture (Mixtures), Reed Stops, Klangfarbe, and others, I have given a few general principles which permit the registration to be varied according to the effect which it is required to produce; I have said that the noble and virile Principal, accompanied by Bourdons, Flutes, and Gambas, lends gravity, majesty, and fullness to the sound; that the Mixtures, the 2′ stops, and the vigorous reed stops lend *éclat* and precision; I have urged the organist first of all to study the 8′ stops of his organ (see below), which form the basis of all registration; finally, I have uttered a warning against an indiscreet use of the tremolo, and those clumsy effects which result from the sudden transition from the full organ to a hardly perceptible pianissimo.

Herzog, in his *Orgelschule*, says that an organist imbued with high-mindedness and with the sacredness of his office will adapt his registration in conformity with the character of the prelude and of the chorale which he is to play, guarding against all excessive display, maintaining a noble simplicity alone worthy of Divine Service.

For further guidance on this point I would refer the reader to Ehrenhofer, Anding, Weipert, Wangemann, Richter, Riemann, Schildknecht, etc.

In an interesting report, Spittel, Court organist at Gotha, writes as follows concerning the rôle of the organ in Divine Service:—" The organ is the church instrument *par excellence* amongst nearly all cults; it has occupied this place of honour for the last ten centuries. Its voice—now soft and humble, now grave, solemn, or enthusiastic—lends itself above all others to the expression of all the sentiments of the faithful—sadness, repentance, praise, adoration: it elevates the soul above the earth in order to let it contemplate the eternal truths."

Doubtless, in order that the organ shall be equal to its exalted task, it is necessary for it to possess a comprehensive and judicious choice of stops, in proportion to the size and acoustic properties of the church in which it is placed. It will be wise, therefore, when a new instrument is required, to consult not only an able builder but also a competent and experienced organist. (See also SPECIFICATION.)

The collective registers, which are now to be found in nearly every organ, and which offer to the organist three or four (or more) combinations to be fixed in advance without any further manipulation, render the art of registration incomparably easier than was formerly the case; but they also fail to stimulate sufficiently the organist into making personal experiments. (See ÆOLINE, COUPLER, and COLLECTIVE REGISTERS.)

It goes without saying, besides, that all the principles that one can lay down with reference to the art of registration are only general and relative, and that a church, an organ, and a piece of music each offer their peculiarities, which must be specially studied.

Herr Musikdirektor R. Löw, organist at Basle, wrote me these excellent lines:—" The same combination which, in St Elisabeth's Church, for instance, would be beautifully effective, might not be so successful in the Cathedral, and *vice versa.*" Every organ must therefore be studied specially (see KLANGFARBE); only general principles can be laid down, without entering into details, and often a certain stop-combination which, at first, seems almost impossible, may produce, under certain circumstances, an excellent effect.

I have also found in Pirro's work, *L'Orgue de J.-S. Bach,* an excellent chapter dealing with the master's method of registration. (English and German translations of this excellent work have been published. —TR.) I append a few summary and practical rules furnished by the eminent Berlin organist, Herr Otto Dienel, especially for this book:—

"If one blends together the stops of the same group, the following homogeneous combinations will result: (1) Principal stops; (2) Flutes and Bourdons; (3) Gambas and Salicionals, representing the 'strings';

(4) Reeds; (5) Mixtures, belonging to the fortissimo. Pedals acting upon these different groups are found, for instance, in the new concert-organ in the Vienna Musiksaal (Rieger). But beautiful effects may also be obtained by blending stops of different families (see COUPLER). It must be remembered that 4', 2' and $2\frac{2}{3}$' stops and mixtures only accentuate the harmonics, little represented in 8' stops, and that 16' stops reinforce the 8' stops in the lower octave."

I have already said—and here repeat—that first of all one must study thoroughly all the various tone-colours (" Klangfarben ") of the 8' stops, which are the basis of all registration.[1] The other stops should be used solely to colour the latter, so to speak.

Finally, one must further take into account the various degrees of intensity of stops of different families, and I cannot urge too strongly the organist to compare them between themselves, to study his instrument in detail, so as to get to know it, so to speak, by heart. (See also KLANGFARBE, ÆOLINE, and COUPLER.)

[1] Already in 1618, Prætorius, in his *Syntagma* (vol. ii. chap. 4), characterises in a very original manner the importance of the 8' stops in the organ:—" The 8' stops are the most agreeable of all, and those which resemble more closely the human voice and the most commonly known instruments; they possess a mysterious and inexplicable charm; they take from the shrillest stops all their little imperfections, to elevate them to the purity and the nobility which they themselves possess." See also what the celebrated organist, Ch. M. Widor, says about these stops in the preface to A. Pirro's work on J. S. Bach (p. 31: Paris, Fischbacher).

I cannot refrain from citing the following passage from Anthe's *Die Tonkunst*:—"The high aim of all sacred music is to elevate the soul to God; this is particularly the aim of organ music. Majesty and elevation are the laws from which it should never depart."

An organist imbued with the grandeur and the sacredness of his task may, according to the means at his disposal—now powerful, now soft,—elevate the souls of the faithful above the preoccupations of this world, contribute to their edification, and engender in them good resolutions.

The historic Nydeck organ in Berne bears the following inscription in gilt letters on the front: *Soli Deo Gloria*; upon the organ in St Mary's, Lübeck, we read: *In excelsis Gloria Deo*; upon the magnificent front of the Haarlem organ (see PRESTANT): *Vincit vim virtus* ("Virtue conquers strength"). Finally, the following quotation from the Bible has been engraved upon Silbermann's organ at Schneeberg (Saxony): *Singet dem Herrn ein neues Lied!* ("Sing to the Lord a new song").

Hints for very effective registration appear also under FUGARA, GEIGENPRINCIPAL, CLARINET, TRUMPET, FLAUTO TRAVERSO, VOIX CÉLESTE, OCTAVE COUPLER (close of article), etc.

Nowadays, organ-builders make special efforts and surpass themselves in inventing the most ingenious combinations and facilitating the organist's task in every direction. Such an ambition is certainly deserving of all praise; but in everything excess is deplorable; and I fully agree with a number of eminently competent colleagues who declare that it is perfect drudgery to have to play an organ surcharged with over-complicated improvements. (See PNEUMATIC BUTTONS, COLLECTIVE REGISTERS, and CONSOLE.)

Ripieno. See MIXTURE.

Röhrenpneumatik (Tubular Pneumatic). See PNEUMATIC.

Rohrflöte (*Fr.*, Flûte à cheminée) is a covered flue stop, either 8′ or 4′, the lid of which is provided with a chimney (*röhre*, fig. 11), which imparts to the tone a peculiar, rather brighter character. The width of this little tube depends upon its length, both dimensions increasing or decreasing together. The widest must therefore be almost as long as the flue itself (*vide* Töpfer, vol. i. p. 79).

The power and brightness of the tone increase as the tube widens, while if the tube be too narrow the tone can scarcely be distinguished from that of a Gedackt.

In Silesian organs—*i.e.* on the 2nd manual of the Breslau Cathedral organ—double-lipped Rohr flutes are to be met with.

In small organs the Rohrflöte sometimes takes the

place of the Gedackt on an upper manual, if otherwise the flute character be too feebly represented. Both stops may also appear very well side by side. Anyhow, a Rohrflöte should by rights always be secondary to the 8′ Bourdon, and should only be employed when the latter stop is omitted.

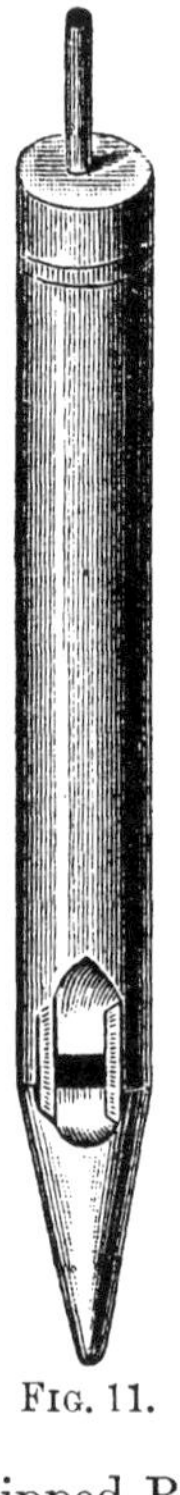

A very characteristic effect is obtained by combining a Bourdon 8′ and a Rohrflöte 4′ with a Viola 8′ (enclosed). Another happy combination results from the union of a Rohrflöte 4′ with a fine cutting Gamba 8′ and a Dolce 8′, or (where the 1st manual possesses a Rohrflöte) by coupling it with a Clarinet or an Oboe capable of dynamic treatment. The union of a Salicional with the Rohrflöte is also very effective, *e.g.*, in the fine organ at Brienz (Bernese Oberland). The Rohrflöte 8′ also combines agreeably with the Flûte d'Amour 4′, which imparts brightness to it. (See also REGISTRATION.) A fine Rohrflöte 16′ is found on the swell of the organ at Sarnen (Goll); and a double-lipped Rohrflöte 4′ at Schweidnitz (Schlag & Sons).

FIG. 11.

Rohrquinte. See QUINT.

Rohrwerk. See REEDS.

Rollschweller. A roller worked by the foot, and

lately also by the hand, by means of which all the stops, from the Æoline to the full organ, are gradually brought into play, and which I would recommend also for the smaller organs. My recommendation has found echo even in Central Russia, where, in an organ erected by Wilhelm Sauer at Nijni-Novgorod, containing but eighteen stops, the specification called for a Rollschweller in addition to a swell-box for the 2nd manual. (For reasons explained below, I express a decided preference for the roller as against the balanced pedal.)[1]

The new organ in the Wallfahrtskirche at Kevelaer contains, in addition to the above-described Rollschweller pedal, a hand-lever, affixed to the left of the console, which allows the manipulation of the crescendo by an assistant, and serves, at the same time, as swell-indicator for the position of the swell-shutters. For the choir organ there is, in addition, a balanced pedal.

A Rollschweller for each family of pipes is advantageous, if the succession of stops is aptly carried out, and especially if the transition to the mixtures is a progressive one, and, lastly, if the installation of the

[1] As this is one of the most practical of mechanical aids to playing (*vide* repeated mention of the Vienna Congress elsewhere in this book), I would draw attention to the excellent elucidation of the results of the application of this contrivance in the technical journal *Die Orgel*, by Prof. Arthur Egidis, whose admirable hints have greatly contributed to enlightenment on organ matters.

whole leaves nothing to be desired from a technical point of view. But it must be arranged conveniently.

In the 113-stop organ in Berlin Cathedral, and since then in numerous other organs, I found the Rollschweller in the middle, as well as three crescendo pedals situated on the right-hand side, very conveniently arranged, and in such a manner that the left foot, which in modern organ-playing is so much required, is able to work entirely unfettered.

Often one meets with organs in which extraordinary gymnastic exercises are expected of the right foot in the use of the crescendo pedals, which are too far off. In organ contracts, therefore, the purely technical comfort of dynamic accessories should be prescribed and strictly regulated. In order to indicate the amount of power attained by the use of the Rollschweller, one frequently meets, nowadays, with a contrivance consisting either of ivory buttons which come out or retract, or of coloured lights indicating the stops drawn into use. This contrivance specially serves the purpose of defining clearly the well-known stop-indicators. The reader is also referred to the article by Max Allihn on accessories to playing, published in the *Z. f. I.*, and to the essay on *Modern Art of Organ-building* by the Bros. Rieger.

Rückpositiv. German builders employ this term to designate a small portion of an organ placed opposite to the main portion of the instrument, the organist being between the two. Such "Rückpositive" are often met with in old instruments. But I have also found them in recent instruments, *e.g.* in the new Berlin Cathedral organ (Sauer), where the Rückpositiv answers to the 3rd manual, and can be connected with the main instrument by means of a convenient pedal placed by the side of the Rollschweller. This Rückpositiv comprises a group of Flutes, together with a Gedackt 8′ and a Dulciana. Some very fine effects may be obtained by suddenly introducing this *ensemble* of flutes into a combination of string-toned stops.

S

Salicet. See SALICIONAL.

Salicional or **Salicet.** Is one of the most popular organ-stops, and belongs to the Gamba family. It is made as 16′, 8′, and 4′, rarely as 2′ (*e.g.* Riga Cathedral). Its scale is sometimes a little larger than that of the Gamba, in which case its tone is a little less "biting."

The late Hoforganist Gottschalg, of Weimar, wrote me that, in the north of Germany, the scales of the Gamba and Salicional are often reversed. Seidel and Zamminer derive the word Salicional from the Latin *Salicis fistula* (willow-flute). (See FISTULA.)

Formerly the Salicional, on account of the construction of its pipes, was somewhat slow of speech.

Nowadays, however, the improvements in organ-building have done away with this imperfection. (See GAMBA.) The largest pipes of this stop are often constructed of wood. (See ÆOLIAN HARP.)

As a pedal stop, it sometimes bears the name of Salicetbass 16′ (*e.g.* St Michael's, Hamburg; Pilsen; Nicolaikirche, Leipzig; Gedächtniskirche, Berlin) or simply Salicional 16′ (St George's Hall, Liverpool). The Salicional 16′ closely resembles the Harmonica-bass 16′ (*q.v.*). Compare also Gambenbass in the article GAMBA. A delicate 2′ pedal stop, under the designation of Salicet, has lately been placed in St Michael's, Hamburg. Double-lipped Salicionals are also to be met with in Sweden. I am indebted to the organist Hennerberg, of Stockholm, for some very valuable information concerning Swedish organs.

The Salicional, which for this purpose should replace the more often used Æoline, is sometimes tuned so as to produce a slight beat, with the Voix céleste (*q.v.*). In this manner some nice effects may be obtained. In all small organs where but one representative of the string family of stops can be included, the Gamba 8′ is often replaced by the Salicional 8′, when this stop is made more " biting."

The Salicional is one of the stops which offer a number of charming combinations. I would mention only its combination with the Flauto Dolce and the Gedackt; or, if a brighter tint be desired, with the Flauto Traverso 4′ or the Flûte d'Amour 4′. In three-manual organs containing a large number of stops, I would strongly recommend placing a Salicional 16′ on the 2nd manual.

The Lieblich-Gedackt 16′, Salicional 8′, Æoline 8′, Geigenprincipal 8′, and Fugara 4′, combined with this and enclosed in an effective swell, yield some wonderful effects. One should bring out the melody, in the above combination, by means of the melodic coupler, employing a fine Bourdon 8′ (enclosed) or a soft Doppelflöte—a suitable pedal to be added. In the new Jerusalem Church at Berlin, Sauer has placed three 16′ Salicionals—on the 1st and 2nd manuals, respectively, and on the pedal as Salicetbass 16′, in addition to a Dulciana 8′. As is the case with the Æoline, it is necessary to couple the Subbass 16′ or Echobass 16′ (Lieblich-Gedackt) with this stop, these delicate Gamba stops lending to the bass beautiful and discreet precision. Also, in the article COUPLER (*q.v.*), I have recommended organ-committees to insist upon the use of pedal couplers to each manual.

The Salicional is one of the stops which best lend themselves to studies in tone-colour, and these should be carried out in the manner suggested in the article ÆOLINE (see also VOICING).

Santflöte. See VIENNA FLUTE.

Scale (*Ger.*, Mensur; *Fr.*, Perce). From the Latin *metior*, to measure; *mensura*, a measure. The MS.

of the eleventh century, mentioned under FISTULA, gives proportions for measurements: " reliquas fistulas ipsius ordinis sic facies ut superiores *gravioris ordinis* fecisti." The expression "scale," frequently used in this work, means all dimensions of organ-pipes—length, width, as well as cutting-up. All these dimensions materially influence the pitch, power, tone-colour (Klangfarbe), and speech of the pipes. The object of making a pipe wide is to obtain a strong, round, thick tone, not easily over-blowing even in the shortest kind of pipe; in addition, wide scales are appropriate to large buildings.

The narrow scale gives a more stringy, incisive, and Gamba-like tone-colour (see also GEIGENPRINCIPAL), a more readily over-blowing tone, and also that particular brilliancy and acuteness peculiar to certain stops; it is suitable, under certain conditions, for small buildings, and for such upper manuals as make no pretence to fullness of tone.

Schalmei (*Fr.*, Chalumeau). A very soft reed stop, mostly 8′, *e.g.* in the Berlin Garnisonskirche. In French organs, it is present generally under the designation of Musette (*e.g.* in the Madeleine, Paris). Zamminer (p. 228) gives a quaint description of this ancient stop (originally a flat tube of green willow bark blown with the lips). According to this authority, the origin of the modern bassoon, clarinet, and oboe is traceable to the Chalumeau, which was used by the Alpine shepherds. The stop appears as Chalumeau 8′ on the 3rd manual of the Hoforgel at Dresden (Silbermann), and as Schalmei 4′ on the 1st pedal-board (see HOHLFLÖTE) of the organ at Lübeck. Sauer often constructs this as a flue stop, although he voices it so as to resemble a reed stop. This makes for facility in tuning. (Berlin, Kaiser Wilhelm Gedächtniskirche and St Paul's; Willibrordi; also in the Gürzenich and Görlitz concert organs.)

I have found the Chalumeau 8′ in nearly all large organs in the Netherlands, and as a 4′ beating reed in St Michael's, Hamburg.

Scharf, Scharff (Sharp). A three- or five-rank mutation stop, to be distinguished from the Mixture (Fourniture) proper in that it contains the Tierce as an intermediate tone. Thus, the three-rank Scharf will be made up as follows: *c e g* or *c e c*; the four-rank, *c e g e* or *g c e c*; the five-rank, *g c e g c*. This stop is well represented in the Saalbauorgel at Frankfurt a. M., and especially so in the Berne Cathedral organ. It is used only with the full organ. It is occasionally to be met with under the Latin designation of Acuta (see also MIXTURE). This vigorous stop should be incorporated only into a rightly conceived and properly balanced specification.

Schweizerflöte (*Fr*. Flûte suisse; Swiss Flute). An obsolete 8′ stop. In spite of its name, this stop belonged to the Gamba family, *e.g.* on the Great manual of the Magdeburg Cathedral organ, where it fills the function of a powerful Gamba. The pipes of this stop were of narrow scale (see Prætorius, *Syntagma*, vol. ii. pt. 4, ch. 2). Ritter also refers to the Schweizerflöte as a string-toned stop with a well-pronounced "bite," especially suitable for large churches.

The name of Swiss Flute—any more than that of Vienna Flute (*q.v.*)—has nothing to justify it from an etymological point of view; and nowhere have I met with it in Switzerland. *Per contra*, I have found it in the organ in Schmalkalden Castle (Germany).

Schwell-Anzeiger. A contrivance fixed to the console, and which allows the organist to see the number of stops employed at any particular moment. It is indispensable in organs possessing a Rollschweller (*q.v.*).

Schwingungen (Vibrations), whole and half. See OCTAVE.

Septime (*Fr.*, Septième; Seventh). A somewhat rare stop. The various organ-builders whom I have consulted have expressed varied opinions regarding its value and effectiveness. More attention, however, has lately been given to this characteristic accessory stop. In Notre-Dame, Paris, there are three Septièmes:

one, $4\frac{4}{7}'$, on the pedal; the others, $2\frac{2}{7}'$ and $1\frac{1}{7}'$, respectively, on the manuals. The same number I found in the organ of 131 stops in the Church of the Trinity at Libau (Russia). The Grossmixtur in the Rudolphinum organ at Prague (Sauer) contains a Septime $2\frac{2}{7}'$; and the interesting Silbermann organ at Schneeberg (Saxony), presided over by Robt. Frenzel (whom I would here take the opportunity of thanking for some valuable information), contains a $2\frac{2}{7}'$ Septime on the Great manual, and a $7\frac{4}{7}'$ on the pedal. Finally, I would mention a very effective three-rank Septime on the Great manual of the organ in Brunswick Cathedral (Furtwängler & Hammer). In the Berlin Cathedral organ, I found an effective Septime $2\frac{2}{7}'$ on the pedal, agreeable even when employed with all the flue stops; this characteristic stop has been included in the pedal department of the organ in St Michael's, Hamburg.

The famous Paris organist, the late Prof. Dr Alexander Guilmant, was kind enough to furnish me, for the purpose of the present work, with some new and valuable information concerning this somewhat peculiar stop. I herewith reproduce M. Guilmant's words:—

"I am of the opinion that mutation stops are equivalent to the colours on a painter's palette, and that a large instrument should contain them all. The Septième completes the series of harmonics and lends great body to the upper notes and to the lower tones, which they reinforce. From a picturesque point of view, one can get some curious effects from its use. This stop should not be included in a specification unless *all* the other harmonics are contained as well, and, I repeat, only in a large instrument and in pro-proportion to the number of the other stops.

"I find that mutation stops are too much neglected in modern organs; they are nevertheless indispensable if one wants to reproduce the older compositions, which are effective only when played with appropriate tone-colour.

"True progress consists in preserving what is good in the organ of the past, adding modern mechanism and stops. And certainly, in our days, stops of exquisite tone have been invented, which are indispensable for the proper rendering of modern music; these also we must have."

Seraphon (*Fr.* and *Eng.*, Seraphone). A stop invented by G. F. Weigle, and described in detail in the *Zeitschrift für Instrumentenbau*, No. 13, 22nd year, which enables one to obtain for flue stops all degrees of intensity imaginable. (See also TUBA MIRABILIS.) In the organ of thirty-three stops built by Weigle for Leut, there are three Seraphones; also the 4th manual of the concert organ of the Vienna "Musikfreunde" Society (Rieger: seventy-one stops) contains a Seraphongamba 4′ and a Seraphonflöte 8′ and 4′. Further, in the detailed specification by Cohen of the organ for the Wallfahrt Church, Kevelaer (Ernst Seiffer), containing also many other interesting features (see CRESCENDO), provision is made for no less than twelve Seraphone stops.

The excellent organ in Christ Church, Mannheim (Steinmeyer), now contains a Seraphonfugara 4′ on the Echo manual.

Serpent 16′ and Bassethorn 8′ (*q.v.*). Two pedal stops of similar scale, built with free reeds, and of soft intonation. They are generally constructed—like the Physharmonica (*q.v.*)—without a tube. They represent the smooth reed-character on the pedal of the Ulm Cathedral organ, and on the swell pedal of the Cathedral organ at Riga. Regarding the relation of these stops to the Ophicleide, see the latter.

Sesquialtera. A two-rank mutation stop frequently found in large organs. Like the Acuta (Scharf), it contains the tierce, but the *upper* tierce. If *c* be touched, the notes *g* and *e* will be heard; the Sesquialtera is therefore composed of the quint and tenth of the ground tone. It is employed only with the full organ. In the organ in the Apostelkirche, Cologne (built by Goll), there are two Sesquialteras on the pedal, $10\frac{2}{3}$′ and $6\frac{2}{5}$′, respectively. (See also MIXTURE, SCHARF, and TIERCE.) A Sesquialtera has been placed on the swell of the new Jerusalem organ at Berlin, and in St Michael's, Hamburg.

In English and American organs, Sesquialtera sometimes designates a kind of "repeating" Cornet, containing from three to six ranks of pipes. If of three ranks, for instance, it gives *e, g, c*.

Sifflöte. A kind of Scharf (Acuta) 1', employed only with the full organ, and found, for instance, in St Mary's, Zwickau (Jehmlich).

Soloclarine. See towards the close of the article TRUMPET.

Sonarpfeife. Walcker calls Sonarpfeife a reedless Clarinet proposed by Seminar Musik-Direktor Trautner, of Kaiserslautern. Through the narrowing and the widening of the passages where the vibration swellings and vibration nodes are formed, the overtones are produced, which are capable of yielding a Clarinet-like tone. I have lately had the opportunity, in Ludwigsburg, of practically testing a successful example of this pipe, which of course lends itself to further experiments.

Specification (or Plan) (from the Latin *disponere*, to establish) is, in short, the plan of the whole organ with reference to its size, strength, distribution, materials, and, above all, the choice and arrangement of the several stops (registers). (See also REED STOPS.)

A well-conceived specification, having regard to the

SPECIFICATION

exigencies of acoustics as well as the size of the building, is the basis upon which rests the success of the whole work. The purely musical question of acoustics and tone-colour should not, in my opinion, be confused with that of system: for it is well known that nearly every organ-builder introduces his own system. Tone-colour and system should therefore be considered as two quite separate aspects of the plan.

There is no doubt, however, that a proportionate reduction of the wind-pressure effects a considerable influence upon the quiet speech and noble intonation stops like the Gedackt. I have referred elsewhere in this book to the credit (here once more acknowledged) due to the learned Strassburg organist, Dr Albert Schweizer, in the planning of an instrument in which he has been good enough to demonstrate personally to me the importance of wind-pressure.

It is in the well-studied interests of a parish wishing to erect an organ, to place the contract only after the important question of the specification has been thoroughly discussed with an experienced organist and an expert of repute.

It is especially advisable that the work be not entered upon hurriedly. There are points arising during the course of negotiations which play a greater rôle in the successful building of an organ than in almost any other enterprise.

It is necessary to point out once more that, in order to facilitate the control of the innumerable aids to playing scattered all over the modern console, the organist should be enabled, by means of contrasts in the colour, form, etc., of the draw-knobs, to see at first glance where he is to look for this or that stop, coupler, etc.

Sperrventil (*lit.*, a "shut-off" valve) is a contrivance found, for instance, in the old organ in Berne Cathedral, which admits and intercepts the passage of wind in the air-trunk by means of a leather-covered valve. It is also used in conjunction with the slide for combining different groups of stops, and is still so employed by Cavaillé-Coll's successors, Merklin, Ladegast, Heinmeyer, and others.

In French organs, for instance, the manuals as well as the pedals have their foundation-stops (Jeux de fonds) and combination stops (Jeux de combinaisons) on different portions of the wind-chest. Accordingly, as the pallet of one or other of the divisions is opened or closed, the combinations of the different groups can be brought into requisition.

Spezialcoppel, **Spezialoctavcoppel**. See COUPLER.

Spieltischanlagen (*Fr.*, Console des Claviers). See CONSOLE.

Spitzflöte (*Fr.*, Flûte à fuseau; *lit.*, a pointed or tapering flute) is a well-known open metal stop resembling the Gemshorn, but somewhat less conical than the latter. Its tone is a little brighter than that of the Flûte d'Amour. The Spitzflöte is often placed on the upper manuals in order to brighten certain 8′ stops of soft intonation; and it appears generally as 4′, more rarely as 8′. Like the Flûte d'Amour (*q.v.*), it is sometimes placed on the principal manual. As regards power, the Spitzflöte is between the Flûte d'Amour 4′ and the Gemshorn 4′, which latter stop it sometimes replaces.

Spitzquinte. A "filling-up" stop $2\frac{2}{3}$′, which has been placed on the 3rd manual of the organ in Magdeburg Cathedral.

Spotted Metal. See GAMBA.

Stentorphon (as a Principal stop). See TUBA MIRABILIS.

Stentor-Sologamba 8′. A stop with a wind-pressure of 200 mm. (about 8 inches) which Walcker has placed in the organ in St John's, Danzig (Op. 1000). The same builder has placed a Stentorgamba as well as a Tuba Mirabilis (which are available either on the Great manual or on the pedal) in the organ in the Evangelical Church at Warsaw, where I found that these two stops complete the well-conceived specification.

Stillgedackt. See GEDACKT.

Stop-keys (Registerclaviatur) instead of Drawknobs (Registerknöpfe). See PNEUMATIC PISTONS.

Suabile. See SUAVIAL.

Suavial (Suave) or **Suabile.** A stop frequently found in old organs. Its tone resembles that of a soft Geigenprincipal 8'. It commences generally from c, e.g. in the organ in the French Church in Berne. I am surprised to find that this beautiful designation has fallen into desuetude.

Subbass (*Fr.*, Soubasse). The name given to a stop 16' or 32' built with covered or "stopped" pipes (see GEDACKT and UNTERSATZ), and found in every organ without exception. In small organs, where the size of the church does not permit the installation of a 16' open pipe, the Subbass is indispensable (even side by side with such an open pipe).

In larger organs with an adequate pedal-department I would recommend the joint employment of the Subbass and Harmonicabass (*q.v.*), which latter stop is of especial value in discreetly lending precision to the sombre fullness of the Subbass.

In both large and small organs the Subbass forms one of the most essential stops; and even in the smallest instruments a mere pedal to Great coupler should not be deemed a sufficient substitute.

From an acoustical point of view, it is worth mentioning that my experience of the character of this stop is, that often the same note, which in one part of the church may be quite powerful, may be scarcely audible a few paces from the same spot. This acoustic peculiarity of the Subbass (and of the lower tones of other stops) has caused no end of trouble to organ-builders, and often made the satisfaction of experts questionable.

Prof. Dr. Forster, of Berne, writes to me on this subject as follows: "It would be doing the organ-builder a great injustice if one attributed this phenomenon to a faulty construction of the instrument. In different parts of the church, increase and decrease in the tone, especially if this be of great length of undulation and of great intensity of direct and reflected waves,[1] may arise from resonance as well as from interference.[2] The appearance of these phenomena is dependent upon the shape and proportions of the interior of the church."

[1] If in an enclosed space a sound is produced, the waves of sound progress in all directions, beating against the walls, from which they are then reflected. The angle of reflection is that which is formed by a vertical line erected at the point struck by the ray of sound, and by the reflected ray itself.

[2] If two or more stones are thrown into still water at different points, two or more systems of rings are formed, which in expanding meet. This meeting—that is, the phenomenon occasioned by it—is called interference. (See Blaserna, *Theorie des Schalles*, pp. 36 *et seq.*) Beyond the point of meeting the waves proceed undisturbedly the same as before.

The Professor has been good enough to prove to me *ad oculos*, by physical experiments, this explanation, which is as clear as it is concise.

With reference to the acoustics of enclosed spaces in general, the measurement of the intensity of direct sound, the duration and intensity of resonance, I would further refer the reader to the essays which Prof. Exner, of Vienna, has published in the *Musikalische Wochenblatt*.

The science of acoustics offers a quantity of remarkable facts and phenomena.

The experiments of Dr. Epstein in the physiological laboratory at the University of Berne—experiments which I have kindly been allowed to witness—demonstrate that acoustic phenomena exert a considerable influence upon the visual faculty.

It seems proved that a phenomenon which affects the hearing renders the visual faculty not only keener but more intensive. A consonance, it would appear, would augment this faculty, whilst a dissonance would diminish it.

Dr. Epstein read an interesting paper on "The Modification of Visual Perception under the Influence of Sound" at the International Physiological Congress which took place in Berne, at the Physiological Institute of the University, whose Director, Prof. Dr. Kronecker, as well as his colleague, the late Hermann von Helmholtz, has greatly aided me in the preparation of this work through repeated suggestions and encouraging expressions of goodwill.

Here should be mentioned an apparatus by Professors Martens and C. Leppin, which renders visible tone-vibrations in the form of light-curves. The experiments carried out by Prof. Pauck in the Treptow Observatory, in illustration of his lecture on "Visible Sounds and Sounding-light," have been clearly described in the excellent *Z. f. I.* (Paul de Wit), No. 2, 32nd year. I would further refer the reader to Prof. Dr. Karl Humpf's work, *Tonpsychologie* (Leipzig: Hirzel). It contains some remarkable chapters regarding physiological sensations and the influence of sound upon different individuals—chapters which I would commend to all who desire to delve more deeply into the domain of physiological acoustics.

With reference to these questions of the influence exercised by sound and sonorous waves, I have also corresponded with the learned Dr. Victor Urbantschitsch, of Vienna, who is an authority in such matters; and I would here mention, among others, the extremely interesting researches which he has published in the *Archives of General Physiology* (vols. lii. and lxxiv.). It would appear, for instance, from experiments carried out with a variety of subjects, that the writing of the same person may be modified according to the influence of deep or acute sounds. Urbantschitsch recognises, however, that the subject, by opposing his will, may sometimes weaken or even annul the effect of the experiment.

I have thought it my duty, in a work which repeatedly treats of acoustic sensations, and notably of "Klangtints," not to let pass without mention the original observations to which I have just alluded; and I would herewith express my profound gratitude to the distinguished *savants* who, by their valuable contributions and their encouraging attitude, have been kind enough to lend me their aid.[1]

With regard to the designation Subbass for Principal Bass, see the latter. The Subbass, employed singly, lends itself to the accompaniment of soft stops. As I have already said, its sound may be slightly defined by associating with it the Harmonicabass or—if a stronger bass be required—the Violonbass. The Violoncello defines and reinforces still more. The Bass Flute or the Octavbass lends body and roundness, rather than precision, to the tone of the Subbass (see FLUTE). Further precision may be given to the Subbass by coupling it (either by means of a coupler or by transmission (*q.v.*)) with a stop belonging to the 2nd or 3rd manual (particularly with a fine stringtoned stop). For Grossgedacktbass 32′, see GEDACKT. Here I would draw the reader's attention to the

[1] The essay by Gust. Ad. Buschmann (Hamburg) in No. 8, 52nd year, of the *Z. f. I.*, upon the old experiments with the Glasharmonica, the Terpodion, the Flaschenorgel, the Metallorgel, and, above all, with Chladni's Euphon and Clavicylinder, etc., forms a most interesting study in physical acoustics.

extremely beautiful effects which may be obtained by occasionally coupling the Subbass 16' with the Æoline, the Salicional, and the Dolce (see also ECHOBASS). These string-toned stops—to which an 8' Gedackt may be added in order to render the tone slightly rounder—lend to the Subbass a discreet precision; and, if enclosed in a swell-box, one may impart to the combination a lighter or a darker colouring, according to their greater or lesser predominance. (See COUPLER, REGISTRATION, and SALICIONAL.)

Suboctave Coupler. See TERTIA MANU.

Superoctave Coupler. See TERTIA MANU.

Swell-box. Crescendo or swell pedals are the well-known pedals, usually placed low on the right-hand side, by means of which the shutters of the swell-boxes are opened and closed. It should be arranged that the swell pedal remain stationary at the very point where the foot leaves it, and not proceed further on its own account, and further, that a uniform crescendo results when the foot is pressed forward, and a decrescendo with a retrograde movement of the foot.

Formerly only one or two manuals (with a corresponding number of swell pedals) were enclosed in swell-boxes. To-day three or four swell-boxes are met with, and it is not unusual to find an extra one enclosing the whole organ. Marvellously fine effects may be obtained by the use of such dynamic contrivances, as, for instance, in the concert organ in the Berne Casino, built by Goll. This particular instrument is surrounded by a fine grill-work case which hides the interior from public view—an all the more acceptable arrangement. There are now smaller and larger organs which are entirely enclosed in a single large swell-box. It cannot be denied that a certain individuality is thereby lost to some of the manuals. Therefore, individual swell-boxes should be erected within and without such a general swell-box for the 2nd, 3rd, and 4th manuals, which could then be subject to dynamic treatment without interfering with the general crescendo. In order to obtain this effective crescendo in smaller organs, one should try, for instance with a two-manual instrument, to enclose the whole organ in a single swell-box, enclosing the swell manual in a separate box. If, as in the case of churches (see above), it is not desired to lose the effect of the front pipes, one might provide for the front a set of handsome tin pipes for the Principal, thus strengthening the whole.

The arrangement of the shutters should, where possible, be such that the lids of the shutters open not only sideways and in front, but also upwards and backwards (see VOX HUMANA). This would result in an astonishing improvement of certain characteristic stops, as well as yielding greater dynamic intensity.

A great drawback formerly existed in many swells,

in that they often enclosed a comparatively feeble manual, on which there was practically nothing to increase or diminish.

I would repeat here what I have already said in the article on the Coupler, that parishes building organs—even particularly small ones—containing but few stops, ought not to grudge the small extra cost of a good swell-box, for the 2nd manual, and even for the whole organ (excluding, in the case of churches, the front pipes). Where an organist has only a limited number of stops at his disposal, he is thus enabled to make the most of his resources by means of dynamic enrichments and changes, thus affording pleasure to his hearers even with a small instrument. Dr. Albert Schweizer is quite of my opinion: he advises (*Grazer Z. f. I.*, 5th year), where limited funds impose a choice between one stop more and a swell-box, to sacrifice unhesitatingly the former for the latter; for, he says, " a good swell-box —according as to whether it is open or closed— practically doubles the number of stops in an organ." Already the great Handel and the learned Abbé Vogler were firm partisans of the swell-box (*vide* preface by Widor in Pirro's study on Bach, an excellent German edition of which has recently been published by Schuster & Löffler, of Berlin). The manner of obtaining a crescendo by means of swell-boxes provided with shutters has a certain advantage over the Rollschweller (*q.v.*), in that, with the former, the increase of sound proceeds in a more uniform and uninterrupted manner, whereas even with the best rotary action the chiming in of each successive stop and uniform intensity will be interrupted to a certain extent.

With reference to the excellent effect of enclosed pedal-stops—even the deepest—like, for instance, a Lieblich-Gedackt 32′, see my remarks at the end of article TRUMPET.

Syntematophon. This stop belongs to the Principal (Diapason) order and is voiced loud. The pipes are of metal, of wide scale and conical shape, narrowing towards the top. They are double-lipped, the lips facing each other; the slot is straight. The volume of tone is about four to five times greater than that of an ordinary Principal. Walcker, the builder of the 163-stop organ in the new St Michael's Church, Hamburg, has placed this important high-pressure stop in the 4th manual swell-box of this organ, as well as in that of the Hamburg Musikhalle.

The Syntematophon also forms a leading stop in the ingenious specification of the Dortmund organ, mostly due to the celebrated artist Holtschneider.

T

Temperament (from the Latin *temperare*, to regulate, to bring within bounds, to reduce to just proportions) is the manner, described in detail under OCTAVE (*q.v.*), of deciding the intervals ("laying the bearings"), which, in short, enables us to play relatively in tune in all keys. (See also VOICING.)

Terpodion (from the Greek τέρπω, to rejoice, and ἰρδή, a song), according to Richter, was originally an instrument in which the sound was produced by means of small wooden sticks; according to Schubert, however, an instrument similar to the piano. The word is also employed to designate a kind of flute which figures, for instance, on the 3rd manual of the large organ in St Mary's, Lübeck, and on the 4th manual of the organ in Halberstadt Cathedral. (See also SUBBASS.)

Tertia Manu ("with a third hand"). A kind of coupler which is often found in Italian organs, and which adds to the notes played by the organist those of the corresponding lower or upper octave, and serves to reinforce the full organ and to produce certain characteristic effects. I have found it under the name of Super- and Sub-Octave Coupler in the concert organ of the Stuttgart Liederhalle, and as Octavcoppel in St Peter's, Hamburg. With regard to the now quite indispensable and universally used coupler, Melodic Coupler, and octave couplers of all kinds, see detailed description of these important contrivances under their respective headings.

Tertian. A stop found in fairly old organs, and in which the two pipes forming it lie in inverse proportion, as is the case with the Sesquialtera, *i.e.*, $\bar{\bar{e}}$ and $\bar{\bar{g}}$, and thus form a third: hence the name, "Tertian."

Tibia. See FLUTE.

Tierce (*Ger.*, Terz). A mutation stop with metal pipes, of Principal scale and flute-like character. As its name implies, it yields the major third, *i.e.* when c is pressed down, e is heard. It is found especially in large organs, where it appropriately belongs, but sometimes, like the Quints and Mixtures (*q.v.*), in little village organs. But this constitutes an abuse, where it cannot be supported by an adequate number of foundation-stops. The ordinary dimensions of the Tierce are: $1\frac{3}{5}'$, $3\frac{1}{5}'$, $6\frac{2}{5}'$. A Tierce of unusual dimensions, viz., $12\frac{4}{5}'$, is to be found on the pedal of the organ in the Nicolaikirche at Leipzig and in Schwerin Cathedral. A Gemshornterz (conical) has been placed on the 4th manual of the organ in St Michael's, Hamburg. The Tierce is also the fifth harmonic in the natural scale. As is the case with the Quint (*q.v.*), one must distinguish between the real sound of the Tierce and the place accorded to it in the specification. In the latter, the Tierce contains as many fifths of a foot as the corresponding fundamental tone has whole feet. This stop is employed with the full organ. Happily, those noisy little organs in which Tierces,

Quints, Sesquialteras, and Mixtures predominate, instead of a fine mass of fundamental 8′ tone, are fast disappearing.

Tirasse. The French designation for pedal coupler.

Tonhalle. German builders employ this term to designate an independent chamber constructed in connection with large organs, and generally in the tower of the church, and in which certain stops like Vox Humana, Voix céleste, Echo-Bourdon, etc, are often enclosed. A round opening made in the ceiling of the church and connected with this chamber by a kind of tunnel enables the hearer to enjoy these far-away sounds.

Some beautiful effects may be obtained by the use of a well-voiced Echo-Bourdon 8′, placed in a Tonhalle constructed in accordance with all the principles of acoustics, and accompanied by a good Tremulant. The Echo-Bourdon is equally useful as a corrective for the somewhat metallic sound which the Vox Humana too often possesses.

The beautiful effects which have been lately obtained by means of the Tonhalle in different places, have led to its increasing adoption where circumstances permit it. Thanks to the progress of electricity, of pneumatics, and of electro-pneumatics, the difficulties of distance have been practically abolished. It is highly advisable, especially in the case of so difficult a stop as the Vox Humana, that such a stop should be as far as possible removed from the body of the organ (Fernstation), in order to modify and ennoble, by means of acoustics, the metallic sound which is apt to cling to it. (See Vox HUMANA.)

I found, in the beautiful organ in the Kaiser Wilhelm Gedächtniskirche, Berlin, a remarkably effective Tonhalle. The organ itself is due to the munificence of H.M. the Empress Augusta Victoria. Having had the honour of a private audience at the new palace of Potsdam, I was able to express to the gracious Lady my own and all my colleagues' warmest thanks for the enlightened and generous interest which she has always displayed in all matters pertaining to church and organ-building. The Kaiser Wilhelm Gedächtniskirche organ is a remarkable monument of the art of organ-building.

No less grateful am I to H.M. Margherita, the Queen-Mother of Italy, for her gracious invitation extended to me on the occasion of the appearance of the Italian edition of my work (Milan: Ulrico Hoepli), for which I received her warmest thanks. I mention this solely because Queen Margherita is in a sense a colleague. She has had an organ built for her in her palace, and formerly took lessons from the late Filippo Capocci, organist at the Lateran Church in Rome, and attended the lectures of Professor Pietro Blaserna, the great Roman physicist. After these little personal digressions, I desire equally to express my thanks to the various Ministers of Religion and of Education who have repeatedly signified their approval of my modest work. This has been of great encouragement to me.

Transmission ("Borrowing," in English organ-building parlance). A highly important mechanism due to the progress of the pneumatic system, and which allows every stop on a given manual to be used also on the pedal or on another manual. Judicious transmission can render inestimable service to the player, and can effect a considerable saving. It goes without saying, however, that in large organs, where neither space nor expense need be considered, it is always preferable to have independent stops for both manuals and pedal.

Mention might conveniently be made here of Wittwer's invention, which, by a free employment of the stops, affords a general use of tone-material not previously utilised. The Wittwer system, employed judiciously, is to be recommended in many instances, and has been successfully used by Goll, who, moreover, has improved it. In his excellent work, *Taschenbuch des Orgelrevisors* ("Dictionary of the Organ-Expert") (the *best* of its kind), the Viennese engineer, Edm. Ehrenhofer, draws attention to various systems, all having the same end in view, as, for instance, the various improvements originated by the famous acoustician Joachim Steiner (double manual, twin-manual, multiplex stops, etc.). One may read there the interesting chapters dealing with combination-manuals (Rieger, Mauracher, Schulze, Röver, Hopferwieser, Faber and Greve, and others), and similar information in the *Zeitschrift für Instrumentenbau* (P. de Wit). Many very authoritative readers of the book have earnestly dissuaded me against taking part in the well-known polemic on the subject of certain systems:[1] and they welcome so much more my numerous new hints for effective registration and the employment of modern accessory aids to playing.

Tremulant (*Fr.*, Tremblant; *It.*, Tremolo). The trembling is produced in new organs chiefly by a valve placed in the wind-trunk, and which, with the bellows at rest, presses firmly against the frame of the trunk. When raised by the draw-knob controlling it, it vibrates freely in the air-current and offers resistance by means of springs, which assist the vibration. The Tremulant is a contrivance which at times is strangely abused, in which case it would be much better not to possess it at all (see also Helmholtz, p. 251).

The use of this register has at all times given rise to interesting opinions on the part of experts. I owe

[1] The late Max Allihn, under the terse heading, "Zum Stand der Frage" ("To the Point of the Question"), has left us a very interesting study in the excellently edited and equally useful official organ of the German Organists' Society — *Die Orgel* (Fritz Lubrich).

it to the pen of an authority like Camille Saint-Saëns to be able to render literally the result of a correspondence with him on this very point. Saint-Saëns writes me as follows (by a happy coincidence, on his seventy-fifth birthday):—

"I fully agree with your remarks regarding the stops which I would aptly christen the 'sweetmeats' (*sucreries*) of the organ, *i.e.* Tremulant, Vox Humana, Voix céleste, etc. It would appear to me to be cruel to suppress them altogether—one can never have too many resources at one's disposal,—but their employment should be, in my opinion as in yours, rare and exceptional. Such effects tickle vulgar ears, and on that account artists without taste and conscience are led to abuse of them. I have known some who always used the Tremulant; and these are those who ring the changes on Tremulant, Voix céleste, or Vox Humana. Similar observations can never be sufficiently combated against. . . ." In the same manner as the great Frenchman did the great Stuttgart master, Dr. Faisst, express himself (see UNDA MARIS).

The Tremulant should, as a rule, be employed only with the softest stops of the swell (*i.e.* the Echo-Bourdon, the Æoline, the Salicional (see also VOX HUMANA)), and then only in a judicious manner. Its judicious and tasteful and, in this case, effective use may be trusted to the hands of a master. I heard, for instance, Saint-Saëns himself use the Tremulant in Lausanne. See especially also UNDA MARIS and VOIX CÉLESTE.

An effective Tremulant may also be constructed by means of ventilators provided with wings, which function after the manner of windmills.

Tromba. See TRUMPET. Regarding Trombas placed horizontally, as found in certain Spanish organs, *e.g.* at Seville, see GAMBA and HELIKON or FELDTROMPETE, which are also so arranged at Dortmund and Hamburg.

Trombone. See POSAUNE.

Trompette céleste. A softly intoned Trumpet 8′, introduced by the Belgian builder van Bever in the organ in Notre-Dame, Laeken.

Trompette harmonique. As applied to reed stops, the term "harmonique" refers to a tube of double length which is used for the upper octaves (thus, for the Trompette harmonique, starting from *c*). It is evident that reeds are not "harmonic" in the same sense as the flue pipes of the Flûte harmonique; the larger tube is used, in the former case, to augment the volume and the intensity of the sound, which tend to diminish as the scale ascends, and which would end by being no longer portioned to those of the lower octaves (*i.e.* the Trompette harmonique

8′ in the organ in Saint-Sulpice, Paris, and in the Kaiser Wilhelm Gedächtniskirche, Berlin).

The organ in the English Church at Clarens (Kuhn), and that of the Berne Casino (Goll), each possess a Trompette harmonique 8′ on the Great and on the swell (see SWELL-BOX). See also HARMONIC FLUTE and TRUMPET.

Trumpet 8′ (*Ger.*, Trompete; *Fr.*, Trompette). Tuba 16′, Clarino, Tuba Clarion 4′, Clairon 4′, all have pipes in the form of an inverted cone. Built and voiced by a master, and supplied with tubes of right proportions (see REED STOPS), it is one of the most brilliant stops of the organ, and is decidedly effective.

The Trumpet is one of the stops which best illustrate the progress made by modern builders in voicing. Nowadays it is satisfactory to note, in organs by good makers, Trumpets of a powerful yet softly rounded and agreeable metallic tone, whereas in old organs one often meets with harsh and noisy Trumpets. The Trumpet lends variety to the organ, and modifies the somewhat stiff and monotonous tone-character peculiar to flue stops when used exclusively. As is well known, remarkable services have been rendered by Giesecke in connection with the Trumpet and other reed stops.

Trumpets possessing the above qualities are found nowadays in almost all decent organs. I found, for instance, successful specimens of this stop in Brunswick Cathedral (Furtwängler & Hammer), in the Kaiser Wilhelm Gedächtniskirche, Berlin (Sauer), in the Trocadero, Paris (Cavaillé-Coll), in the Stadtkirche at Esslingen (Walcker), in the Berne Münster (Goll), in Lausanne Cathedral (Kuhn), in the Munich Buchsee organ (Zimmermann), as well as in every organ built by a master-hand.

In the case of large organs, I invariably recommend the placing of a good, brilliant Trumpet 8′ in the furthest swell-box. With an *ensemble* of fairly powerful stops, it is at least possible to effect decent crescendoes. The expense involved by this is nothing compared to the advantage which thereby accrues; and it is certainly to be deplored that even in large organs the swell-box sometimes contains a number of feeble stops. (See SWELL-BOX.)

The Clarino (Clairon) is a small 4′ Trumpet, found not only on the pedal but also (together with an 8′ Trumpet) on one or more of the manuals (*i.e.* Notre-Dame, Paris). In large organs I have found a Clairon 4′ both on the Great and on the pedal; and on the pedal of the Stiftsorgel at Stuttgart and of the organ in Ulm Cathedral I found a Clairon 2′. In the highest manual octave this stop repeats (that is, starts again with the larger pipes), because its continuance up to f^3 would be too difficult. In the Trocadero organ, in Paris, I found a Clairon harmonique 4′. Under the designation of Suloclarine

4′, and together with a Glockenspiel (*q.v.*), this stop has been placed in a separate swell-box in the organ in St Michael's, Hamburg. The same organ also contains a high-pressure Trumpet 4′ called Discanttrompete. In organs which do not possess any of the modern improvements, it is advisable to exclude the Trumpet from the composition pedals, unless there is a chance of tuning the organ regularly— particularly the reeds; otherwise, the Trumpet, when out of tune (see OBOE and REED STOPS), renders the composition stops practically useless. A wellvoiced Trumpet needs no combination to be effective; but I can recommend the melodious, virile tone of a good Principal (Diapason) to reinforce it, and the Bourdon 8′ and 16′, with a Rohrflöte 4′, to impart to it a more tender colour. An imposing effect may also be obtained by accompanying a solo on the Trumpet with the stops of a powerful swell-box, causing them, so to speak, to blend with and answer one another, and — at an opportune moment — to augment the expressive power of the whole, add a Subbass 32′ (open, if possible, so that there shall be no "quint" effect). I have often tried, on very large organs, the combination above named.

Generally a soft Subbass 16′ may be used most effectively in characteristic passages, and at the right moment, if it can be enclosed in a swell-box. Such an enclosed Subbass I myself possess in my beautiful organ in the Berne Casino (Goll). That my view is shared by great masters is proved by a letter which I received from Walcker, who, acting upon my advice, has placed a very soft 32′ Gedacktbass in St Michael's, Hamburg. In this letter Walcker states that my suggestion had been complied with, in that, in addition to the above-named, a fine 32′ metal Principal and a 32′ Grossgedacktbass had been placed in the swell-box of the 4th manual. By this means it is possible for these 32′ stops to effect the softest decrescendo, and therefore furnish an adequate support for the most beautiful and delicate stops of the Fernwerk. See KLANGFARBE and VOICING. See also HARMONIC TRUMPET, TROMPETTE CÉLESTE. With regard to horizontally - built "Feldtrompeten" (Allihn), see HELIKON.

Tuba. A 16′ Trumpet (see TUBA MIRABILIS).

Tuba Mirabilis. This stop is frequently found in concert organs. It is a kind of Trumpet or Trombone 8′, very powerful, round and well defined, without being overpowering. It is generally placed on the Solo manual, which is generally on double (or more) the ordinary wind-pressure. This stop is of extraordinary effect, and may rival in power all the other stops put together.

In the Garden City organ (U.S.A.), built by Roosevelt, and comprising 115 stops, the wind-pressure of the Solo manual is nearly three times that allotted to the Great manual, in the proportion of 10 to $3\frac{1}{2}$.

The Tuba Mirabilis is there properly supported by a vigorous Stentorphon 8′ and a Baritone 8′. In the Trocadero, Paris, I found a Bariton 4′, and in an organ in Amsterdam (Maarschalkerwerd) a Bariton 16′.

In the Westminster Abbey organ the Tuba Mirabilis 8′ has a separate sound-board of its own, and is on heavy wind-pressure.

This stop figures in many large organs. Thus, in the organ at Riga, constructed by Walcker (124 stops), I found, on the Great manual, a Tuba Mirabilis the penetrating power of which is still further augmented by a Cornettino 2′, an uncommon reed stop (found also in St Michael's, Hamburg). Weigle has also placed a Tuba Mirabilis 8′ on the Great manual of the great concert organ in the Stuttgart Liederhalle, where its effect is considerably enhanced by a Stentorphon 8′ (as in the Roosevelt organ previously cited) and a Bass Tuba 16′. The organs in the Cathedrals at Lausanne and Brunswick also possess excellent high-pressure Tubas 8′ on the manuals.

Mention must also be made of the Stentorphon in the Philharmonic Hall, Berlin, in the Munich Kaimsaal, in the Gedächtniskirche at Speyer, and in the Convent church at Einsiedeln.

High-pressure stops have been the object of considerable controversy. Of what I have read on the subject, I would signal out as particularly interesting the remarks of my eminent colleagues Hänlein and Dienel in the *Z. f. I.*

In large French organs one finds Harmonic Trumpets answering to the Tuba Mirabilis (see TROMPETTE HARMONIQUE). Regarding the Seraphon, see article.

Tubason. See BOMBARDE.

Tutti. A register or pedal which brings on the full organ, or all the stops of the same family; thus, Generaltutti (full organ), Labialtutti (flue stops), Rohrwerktutti (reeds). See also REGISTRATION.

Twelfth (*Ger.*, Quint; *Fr.*, Quinte). Walcker has employed this English designation in his organ in St Paul's, Dundee.

U

Unda Maris ("sea-wave"). A flute-like metal stop, tuned a little sharper than another soft stop, and which, in combination with the latter, produces an undulating sound which recalls that of the waves. A judicious use of this and similar stops is evidence of good taste. Camille Saint-Saëns, who, from the very first, has manifested the liveliest interest in this work, has made a valuable contribution to this fourth edition. On the use of the Tremulant, see his trenchant remarks under TREMULANT.

Prof. Zellner, of Vienna, is of opinion that the stops in question—especially the Voix céleste, one of the most popular—may sometimes lend a characteristic effect to certain passages.

An Unda Maris 8′ is found in the Heidelberg organ; in the Nicolaikirche, Leipzig; in the 4th manual swell-box of the new Hamburg organ; and in the Gedächtniskirche organ at Speyer. From these examples it is evident that this stop is now being more widely used. The Sarnen organ contains an Unda Maris; also the organs in the Vienna Musiksaal, in Berlin Cathedral, in the Jerusalemkirche, in Christ Church, Mannheim, and many others.

At any rate, I would advise small parishes, which can afford only a small number of stops on each manual, to include the better-known Voix céleste, which is closely related to the Unda Maris, but never otherwise than in a swell-box (see SWELL, and especially VOIX CÉLESTE) and on an upper manual. I consider at least one 2nd manual absolutely indispensable even in small organs, in view of the modern claims made on organists. I have explained my reasons for this in the article SWELL.

See also what has been said under VOIX CÉLESTE. By the use of this stop, a Tremulant may be dispensed with, at least in quite small organs.

Untersatz (Majorbass) is often met with as a 32′ stopped pipe on the pedal, *e.g.* in the Heidelberg

Stadthalle. For reasons of space and cost, it often replaces a 32′ open stop. It is well represented in the Gürzenich organ at Cologne (Sauer). (See SUBBASS and CONTRABASS.) The Untersatz, when placed on the manual, often bears the name of Bourdon 32′. As such I have found it in the following large organs: Libau (Russia), Riga, Paris, London, Leipzig, Ulm, Sydney, etc. Grand Bourdon 32′, see QUINT. Regarding the placing of a soft 32′ Gedacktbass in the swell, see end of article TRUMPET.

V

Vibrations. See OCTAVE.

Viola (Viole d'Amour; Viola d'Amore). A frequently met with metal stop, 8′ and 4′, of a fine string-tone, which often represents the Gamba family on the secondary manuals. I have found a fine Viola 16′ on the 2nd manual of the organ in the Apostelkirche in Cologne (Goll). Brindley & Foster have built a Viole d'Orchestre for the organ built by them for the capital of Natal, and to which I have already referred. (This stop is, of course, quite common in English organs.—TR.)

The Viola should imitate its orchestral prototype (*Fr.*, Alto; *Ger.*, Bratsche).

It is one of the finest among the solo stops. A fine Viola 4′ is to be found on the 2nd manual of the organ in St John's, Helsingfors (Walcker); also an 8' Viola in the Berne Münster (Haas). Also worthy of mention is the Viola d'Amore 8' which Sauer has placed together with a Violoncello 8' on the pedal of the Willibrordi organ at Wesel. The former stop, used in combination with a Bass Flute 16', produces a fine pedal effect. The Viola may be combined with the same stops prescribed for the Salicional (*q.v.*), than which it is slightly more cutting. The organist may obtain equally characteristic effects by coupling a fine Bourdon 8' to a Viola 8' placed in a swell-box.

One should also try Viola 8', Geigenprincipal 8', Æoline 8', Salicional 16', Clarinet 8', emphasising the melody, by means of a melodic coupler, with a flute-like Gedackt or a fine open Flute, employing also Subbass 16', Echobass 16', Harmonicabass 16', Dolcebass 8', and a soft Bourdon 8' through transmission, all these stops being enclosed if possible; and then allow the different tone-colours (Klangfarben) to emerge separately and judiciously by means of the Crescendo pedal, according to the requirements of musical interpretation.

The Viola is one of the stops which, on account of their characteristic tone, are best fitted to replace reed stops in small organs which very rarely receive the attention of the tuner (see OBOE).

It also belongs to those stops of the string family wherewith the student, by comparing each with an open Flute, may learn to distinguish the different tone-colours. If both stops are enclosed, the experiments become still more interesting.

Viole d'Orchestre. See VIOLA.

Violin Diapason. The English designation for Geigenprincipal (*Fr.*, Principal de Violon). See also DIAPASON.

Violino (Violina). A somewhat sharp metal stop 8′ and 4′, resembling in tone the Æoline or the Geigenprincipal, and met with, for instance, in organs by William Hill, Roosevelt, and Hook & Hastings. As an 8′ stop it is of beautiful effect in the Church of the Holy Trinity at Magdeburg; as 4′, in the Stuttgart Liederhalle and in the Johanniskirche at Bergen (Schlag und Söhne); as 2′, in the Nicolaikirche at Leipzig. Also, in the swell of the organ in Berlin Cathedral, a very effective Violino, very similar in tone to a Fugara. A fine Salicional-like Violino 8′ I found on the 3rd manual of the excellent organ in St John's, Leipzig (Röver). See also DIAPASON.

An Orchestergeige 4′ with a distinctive Gamba-like quality has been placed in the organ in St Michael's, Hamburg.

Violino da concerto. A free-beating reed found in Italian organs, the tone of which is akin to that of the Oboe. It speaks only in the upper octaves.

Violon. A stop so named by Dr. Faisst, who recommends its use in the place of the cutting Violoncello 8′ in cases where the latter stop would not blend well with the other stops of the instrument. It differs from the Violoncello in that its scale is larger than that of the latter stop, and is voiced louder, and its tone is clear and round and of a less pronounced "bite."

This stop is nowadays found in the smallest as well as the largest organs, *i.e.* Colombier (Neuchâtel), Gerzensee (Bern), etc. The name Violon was formerly used in numerous organs in North Germany to designate a similar stop of 8′ tone.

Violonbass. A 16′ stop with wooden pipes, frequently placed on the pedal by the side of the Subbass. Haas has placed this stop, with *metal* pipes (a rare procedure), in the front of the Basle Cathedral organ. The Violonbass is a narrow-scaled stop, the tone of which, agreeably "biting," suggests that of the Contrabass. It blends advantageously with the Subbass 16′ — in cases where the Harmonicabass would be somewhat too feeble, — also with the Bass Flute 8′, and again with the Violoncello 8′. (See also HARMONICABASS. and close of article SUBBASS.)

Violoncello. An 8′ stop corresponding to the Violonbass 16′. It is a very characteristic pedal stop, which, as regards construction, material, and tone, corresponds to the Gamba stops of the manual.

For this stop, like many others constructed of metal, good builders nowadays employ successfully spotted metal, which, owing to the persistent rise in the price of tin, is becoming more generally used. Regarding spotted metal, see GAMBA.

I have found some excellent Violoncelli in all new organs by good builders; it is one of the stops which modern art has brought to remarkable perfection. (See VOICING.)

The Violoncello blends agreeably with the Subbass and the Violonbass (*q.v.*). One should try, for the accompaniment of an enclosed Trumpet, a soft Gedackt 32′, together with a Subbass 16′ and a Violoncello 8′ (all enclosed).

Voicing (*Fr.* and *Ger.*, Intonation—from the Latin *intonare*, to resound; or, in a transitive sense, to cause to sound). Voicing (the real *art* in organ-building, unfortunately so often treated as a minor consideration and paid as such; see REED STOPS) is a term which occurs frequently in this work in the articles on flue and reed stops, and which I will therefore endeavour to define briefly.

The voicing of an organ is one of the most important operations, because the tone (in the real sense of the word) of the instrument depends upon it.

The whole instrument may be well built, the pipes

may be of very good material and very accurately constructed, and yet one may not be able to call the organ excellent if the effect of each single tone, as well as of the general tone, does not correspond in faultlessness to the rest of the work.

The results of masterly voicing are:—

(1) The characteristic timbre of each stop is well proportioned to the successive degrees of the scale.

(2) A prompt and easy speech. Töpfer (vol. i. § 1160) expresses himself happily as follows: "It is generally very difficult to obtain *both* good tone and prompt speech; it is therefore easier to obtain good tone if one is satisfied with slower speech." Gamba, Salicional, etc. (*q.v.*), offer eloquent proof of the progress made in articulation and voicing generally (see also FREIN HARMONIQUE).

(3) The possibility of imparting to the pipe a tone-colour in keeping with its character and designation (see, for instance, TRUMPET, CLARINET, FLAUTO TRAVERSO, OBOE, etc.).

(4) The careful equalisation, throughout the scale, of the degree of sound-volume to suit the building.

(5) The proper "temperament" (see OCTAVE) and thoroughly complete tuning of the organ, which should more correctly come under the head of tuning (see also KLANGFARBE and REED STOPS).

Voix céleste. An 8′ metal solo stop, tuned so as to produce a slight beat with the Æoline, Violino, or

Salicional, and generally employed with the first-named. When built as a separate stop, it allows the use of other soft string stops.

A well-voiced Voix céleste is very useful; when combined with the Lieblich-Gedackt 16′ it lends itself well to solemn chord effects; and in combination with the Quintatön 16′ it is singularly effective. The same organ sometimes possesses two differently voiced Voix célestes; such, for instance, I have found in the splendid Fraumünster organ at Zürich, and on the 3rd and 4th manuals of the Kaiser Wilhelm Gedächtniskirche at Berlin.

In order to slightly emphasise the melody, one should try, by means of the melodic coupler, to employ a fine Dolce 8′ on the 1st manual, together with a Lieblich-Gedackt 16′ and a Voix céleste. Or, by playing on the 1st manual and coupling this to swell super-octave, a beautiful effect will be obtained by drawing a Voix céleste 8′ and a Lieblich-Gedackt 16′ on the 2nd manual—a Physharmonica-like effect, with which may be incorporated a Fernflöte on the 3rd manual, either as a solo stop or as a soft embroidery for the purpose of accompaniment. A suitable pedal-bass may be provided for this combination by an Echobass, Harmonicabass, and, by coupling, a dynamically governable Fernflöte. And here I would lay particular stress on the fact that, for the Voix céleste to be effective, it should be tuned very carefully. Moreover, it should be invariably enclosed, either in a swell-box or in a Tonhalle (*q.v.*).

I am more and more convinced that the Voix céleste should be included even in small organs, where reed stops are not available (see OBOE). It lends variety and expression. Such small organs should also, for the same reason, possess a few string stops of characteristic intonation.

However valuable this stop may be, the organist must know how to employ it so that its use may not degenerate into a sickly sentimentality. Above all, one must condemn the use sometimes made of the Voix céleste to accompany solo voices. It is evident that the singer ought to be really supported by the accompaniment. It would be a pity if the abuse which can be made of this stop should prevent its judicious employment. The same applies to all similar stops, *i.e.* Tremulant, Vox Humana, and Unda Maris (*q.v.*).

I have already mentioned that the Voix céleste blends agreeably with the Lieblich-Gedackt 16′ in solemn passages. If an 8′ stop be used instead, the result will be a lighter colouring. The Lieblich-Gedackt 16′ and 8′, Voix céleste 8′, and a soft 4′ Flute provide a delicious accompaniment to a Flauto Dolce 8′ or a Flauto Traverso 8′ employed as a solo, but this accompaniment should be subject to crescendo or diminuendo at will. (See also ÆOLINE and SALICIONAL.) The Subbass 16′ (coupled) provides a suitable pedal-bass to the above-named combination.

Sometimes the Voix céleste bears the Latin designation of Vox cœlestis. This stop should not be confused with the Vox angelica, which is often constructed as a reed stop, although I have found it as a flue stop 4′ in the Riga Cathedral organ.

Volles Werk (Full Organ; *Fr.*, Plein jeu). The late R. Palme pointed out to me that he often observed how organists, at the indication " Volles Werk," pull out at random all the draw-knobs. It only needs this critical remark to remind the student that the above designation does not necessarily include the use of certain rattling and noisy stops, but a mere partial use of certain groups, in accordance with the character of the piece played.

Here I should like to express my sincere thanks to the excellent Magdeburg Cathedral organist, Prof. Forchhammer, for his kind appreciation of my work. Compare what Adlung wrote in 1758 in his *Anleitung zur Musikgelahrtheit* respecting the misinterpretation of the words " Volles Werk " (A. Pirro, Paris, Fischbacher, p. 137). See also REGISTRATION.

Vox angelica. See VOIX CÉLESTE.

Vox cœlestis. See VOIX CÉLESTE

Vox Humana. An 8′ reed stop, which each builder constructs according to his own methods; and which is supposed to imitate the human voice. In spite of all the artistic care which has been brought into the construction of this stop, it has never been possible to avoid—save, perhaps, in the middle notes—a somewhat nasal and metallic sound.

According to Helmholtz, sound, in reed pipes, is produced by the air which penetrates intermittently, the vibrations of the tongue interrupting the current by successively breaking through the opening closed by the reed (see REED STOPS). A hard and unyielding material, like the brass employed in the manufacture of reed stops, renders the jerks much more pronounced than a supple and flexible material. (See end of article CLARINET regarding the experiments which have been made in the construction of wooden tongues.) It is evidently on this account that a fine natural human voice will always be superior to the finest constructed Vox Humana (see Helmholtz, p. 161). That which can best heighten the effect of the Vox Humana depends upon circumstances foreign to the stop itself: I refer to the case in which it is placed in a separate chamber (see TONHALLE).

The Vox Humana may also be accompanied by a stop of a totally different character; it may be combined with a Lieblich-Gedackt or an Echo Bourdon on the swell, together with a discreet use of the

Tremulant, Crescendo pedal, etc. (see my hints in the article FLAUTO TRAVERSO). For a pedal accompaniment to this combination, the Lieblich-Gedacktbass 16′ and 8′, and (by means of a coupler) an Æoline to lend soft precision, render excellent services, assuming always that these stops are capable of being dynamically controlled. In large churches and concert-rooms an intensified crescendo may be further obtained by the use of a soft Grossgedacktbass 32′ for a short time, and with the swell shutters barely opened. It is hardly necessary to point out that I abstain from discussing the various acoustic factors to which this or that Vox Humana may owe its reputation. I am of the opinion that the architecture of the church, the choice of music, the *savoir faire* of the organist, the disposition of the hearer[1] more often contribute to the success of a Vox Humana than all the ability of the organ-builder (cp. Du Hamel's *L'Art du facteur d'orgues*).

In any case, I would recommend my honourable colleagues who have a Vox Humana on their organ to listen personally, from different points of the church or concert-room, to the effects of this stop played in various parts of the scale and with different degrees of intensity, and also to study and compare the

---

[1] As this is evidently a case of momentary inner perception of tone-quality, and therefore a tone-phenomenon, I would refer the reader to the extremely interesting work by Dr. Carl Stumpf, *Tonpsychologie* (Leipzig: Hirschel). See also SUBBASS.

different means of its employment which I have recommended above. Above all, a Vox Humana—if it is not to become grotesque—must be tuned to perfection each time it is used.

W

Waldflöte 2′ is a stop of wide scale, with a strong fluty tone, to be found in large organs (*i.e.* Riga; St Michael's, Hamburg; Kreuzkirche, Dresden; Bern, Luzern, Winterthur). Its lower pipes are frequently made of wood; the higher ones of metal (see FLAUTINO). In the Magdeburg Cathedral organ it is effectively placed as a 4′ stop.

Waldhorn. An 8′ beating reed placed, for instance, in the organ in Passau Cathedral.

Weitpfeife. See FLAGEOLET.

Wienerflöte (Vienna Flute; *Fr.*, Flûte viennoise) is one of the most charming wood flutes, voiced rather brighter than the Flauto Dolce. It appears in numerous specifications, and is generally placed on one of the upper manuals as an 8′ or 4′ solo stop, where it might with equal correctness be called Concert Flute, as I have found it at Mühlhausen. Or it may also be called Deutsche (German) Flöte, as in St Michael's, Hamburg; or Zartflöte and Sanftflöte.

Labelled thus, it occurs as 4′ and 8′ in the Nicolaikirche, Leipzig.

The designation Wienerflöte lacks all etymological or historical foundation (see also SCHWEIZERFLÖTE (Swiss Flute)). In the new Votivkirche organ, although this stands in Vienna itself, there is not a single Wienerflöte amongst its sixty-one speaking stops. The builder of this organ has, however, placed a Wienerflote on the 3rd manual of the organ in Riga Cathedral, and on the swell manual of the Esslingen organ, in order to satisfy the increasing demand for a stop of this name. This is one of the most useful stops on the upper manuals, not only as a solo, but also in combination with any other stop. I have found it particularly beautiful in combination with the swell Oboe and Flauto Traverso (see SWELL-BOX), accompanied by the Lieblich-Gedacktbass 16′ and Harmonica 8′ on the pedal.

In organs containing a Flauto Dolce 8′ on the 1st manual, couple this stop to a fine Wienerflöte or other analogous stop in the swell, and, in order to brighten the effect, add sometimes a small 4′ flute, which latter should, however, be also enclosed, so as not to predominate. If a less bright colour be desired, a Lieblich-Gedackt 8′ may be added. See also REGISTRATION.

Windzeiger (Wind - indicator). A contrivance fixed to the console, which allows the organist to see the increase or decrease of the wind-supply.

Z

Zartflöte (*lit.*, "a tender flute"). A name given by German builders to a flute of very soft and mellow intonation, variously constructed, with wooden flue pipes, by different builders. It appears more often as 8' and 4', more rarely as 2', as in the Gedächtniskirche, Berlin. It lends itself to the same combinations as the Wienerflöte (*q.v.*, also FLUTE). One should try a Zartflöte 8' with Viola 8 and Lieblich-Gedackt 16', with Harmonicabass 16' in the pedal, together with a borrowed soft 8' stop.

Zartgedackt. See GEDACKT.

Zartgeige (*lit.*, "a tender violin"). An 8' flue stop of mellow intonation found together with an Æolian Harp 4' in Passau Cathedral.

Zinnpfeifenmaterial (Metal pipe-material). See GAMBA.

Conclusion

My work treats, above all, of the more or less successful characteristics of the organ-stops.

I take the liberty of concluding my work with a quotation from a rare manuscript which I had the opportunity of examining, through the kindness of Fr. Norbert, Librarian of the Convent at Einsiedeln, wherein, not less than a century back, the learned Fr. Jakob Briefer [1] wrote as follows:—"The character and timbre which the various stops of the organ should possess depend upon the ability of the builder and the care which he brings into his work; for, in a great many organs, certain stops do not come up to the rightful expectations of a connoisseur." I am happy to be able to state here that this reproach—which is not a new one—cannot apply to those among the builders of the present day who are really masters of their craft.

I would again point out that the successful reputation of an organ—independently of the builder's merits—depends largely upon the architecture and acoustic properties of the church or concert-room, the judicious choice of pieces, the ability of the organist, and the disposition of the hearer.　　　　　　　　　　C. L.

---

[1] Regarding this learned artist, see a leading article in the *Schweizerische Musikzeitung*, 41st year, No. 2: "Pater Jakob Briefer, ein Orgelgelehrter des Stiftes Einsiedeln (Beitrag zur Orgelkunde des 18. Jahrhunderts)," by Carl Locher.

A SHORT SKETCH OF THE ART OF ORGAN-BUILDING IN ENGLAND

A BOOK on organ-building, intended for English readers, would be incomplete without some reference to the rise and progress of the art in this country. The subject, however, has been treated at length by far abler pens than mine in existing treatises. England is nothing if not the land of the organ, which, judging by the endless and intelligent discussions going on in the musical papers, appears to have a particular fascination for both amateur and professional musicians. And rightly so; for, is not the organ "the king of instruments"?

Of the excellence of the work of most English builders there would appear to be no doubt. But I may be forgiven if I say that, in organ-building, as in all other matters, England is apt to be too conservative. Conservatism is too often construed to mean "pig-headedness." I speak with some knowledge in the matter, having travelled extensively both on the Continent and in the United States of America and the West Indies. Mr. E. H. Lemare and Mr. Gatty Sellairs, as well as other eminent organists and experts, have written at various time on matters connected with organ-building, such as the desirability of the extension of the manual-compass to five octaves, the standardisation of measurements, etc. To take only one point, viz., the extension of the manual-compass to five octaves. Mr. Hutchings, the head of the Hutchings-Votey Co., of Boston, U.S.A. (whose work was formally recognised by Yale University by the conferment of an honorary M.A. degree), told me some years ago that his *first* organ—erected some forty years ago—was of five-octave manual-compass, with a thirty-note pedal-compass. Yet one has only to look through the specifications appearing regularly in our musical papers, to find that some English builders are still content to go on building organs with a G or an A compass—I presume with the sanction of those who draw up the specifications. The advisability of a five-octave manual-compass is (or should be) undisputed. Here and there one meets with notable specifications, exhibiting signs of progress; but I fear that such are the exception rather than the rule.

The history of organ-building in this country, beginning with John Roose, Antony Duddyngton, and continuing with the Dallams, John Loosemore, "Father" Smith, Renatus Harris, Christopher Schnider, Thomas Schwarbrook, Richard Bridge, John Byfield, the Jordans, John Snetzler, Samuel Green, John Avery, and the Englands, carries us to the eighteenth and nineteenth centuries, with which are associated the honoured names of C. S. Barker, Bryceson, Elliot & Hill (William Hill & Son), Bishop & Sons, Gray & Davidson, Bevington, Flight &

Robson, "Father" Willis, Jos. Walker & Sons, T. C. Lewis, Henry Jones & Son, Jardine & Co., P. Conacher & Co. It is pleasurable to note that to this long and unbroken line of sterling craftsmen must be added, in recent times, the names of Robert Hope-Jones and J. T. Austin (both of whom are doing excellent work in the U.S.A.), Thomas Casson, Foster & Andrews, Brindley & Foster, J. Binns, Hele & Co., August Gern, R. Spurden Rutt, Norman & Beard, Ltd., Rushworth & Dreaper. This long list of names is eloquent in itself; no doubt many other names of firms not so well known as those mentioned above, but whose output, if limited in quantity, is nevertheless of excellent quality, might be made to swell the list.

The important subject of blowing, too, is receiving due attention; and mention might be made of the firms of J. H. Taylor, the Rotasphere Co., the Kinetic Co., Watkins & Watson, whose efforts in providing steady and silent blowing apparatus, utilising electricity, gas, and water, according to the requirements of each case, are meeting with deserved success.

It would be both idle and invidious for me to point out examples of notable organs in this country: they are to be found everywhere; and there are numerous treatises containing numberless specifications.

All that one may now ask for is the hearty and intelligent co-operation of organists, experts, and builders in producing not monstrosities, but specifications which shall exhibit some uniformity of standard (especially in the matter of measurements) and facilitate the player's task, which, never an easy one, nowadays seems to increase in severity.

C. P. L.

INDEX

Accentcoppel, 1.
Acoustic Phenomena, 1.
Acoustic Tones, 1.
Acuta, 1.
Æoline, 1.
Æolian Bass, 4.
Æolian Harp, 4.
Aliquot, 4.
Amorosa, 4.
Ausschaltungen, 4.
Auswechslung, 4.
Auszug, 5.

Baarpijp, 5.
Baritone, 5.
Bass Flute, 5.
Bass Tuba, 5.
Bassethorn, 5.
Bassoon, 5.
Bassoon-Oboe, 6.
Bauernflöte, 6.
Bell Gamba, 7.
Bifara, 7.
Bombarde, 7.
Bombardon, 8.
Bordun, Bourdon, 8.
Bourdonbass, 9.

Calcant und Gebläsemotoren, 9.
Campanelli, 14.
Cardboard, 14.
Carillon, 14.
Cello, 16.
Chalumeau, 16.
Choralbass, 16.
Clairon, 16.

Clarabella, 16.
Clarinet, 17.
Clarino, 19.
Clavaeoline, 19.
Clochette, 19.
Collective Coupler, 19.
Collective Pedals, 19.
Collective Registers, 20.
Collectiv-Schweller, 20.
Combination Registers, 20.
Concert Flute, 21.
Console, 22.
Contrabass, 23.
Contragamba, 23.
Contra-Harmonicabass, 23.
Contraposaune, 24.
Contraviolon, 24.
Coppelflöte, 24.
Copplung, 24.
Cor anglais, 24.
Cor de nuit, 25.
Cormorne, 25.
Cornet à piston, 25.
Cornet harmonique, 26.
Cornett, 26.
Cornettin, 27.
Cornettino, 27.
Corno, 27.
Cornopean, 27.
Coupler, 28.
Crescendo, 30.
Cymbal, 30.
Cymbelstern, 30.

Deutsche Flöte, 30.
Diapason, 30.

Differential Tones, 31.
Discanttrompete, 31.
Disposition, 31.
Dolce, 31.
Dolciano, 33.
Dolcissimo, 33.
Doppelflöte, 33.
Doppelpedal, 34.
Doppelrohrflöte, 34.
Doublette, 34.
Drucknöpfe, 34.
Dulcian, 34.
Dulciana, 34.
Dulcianbass, 35.

Echo, 35.
Echobass, 36.
Echocornett, 36.
Echo Gamba, 36.
Echomixtur, 37.
Echowerk, 37.
Electricity, 37.
Electro-pneumatic action, 37.
Euphonia, 42.
Evacuant, 43.

Faberton, 43.
Fagott, 43.
Feldpfeife, 43.
Feldtrompete, 43.
Fernflöte, 44.
Fernstation, 44.
Fifteenth, 44.
Fistula, 44.
Flachflöte, 45.
Flageolet, 45.
Flautino, 45.
Flauto Amabile, 46.
Flauto Dolce, 46.
Flauto Major, 47.
Flauto Piccolo, 47.
Flauto Traverso, 47.
Flötenprincipal, 49.
Flue Stops, 49.

Flute, 54.
Flûte à Cheminée, 56.
Flûte d'Amour, 56.
Flûte Octaviante or Harmonique, 56.
Fourniture, 56.
Free Combinations, 57.
Frein harmonique, 57.
Fugara, 57.
Fusswalze, 58.

Gamba, 58.
Gambenbass, 64.
Gebläsemotoren, 65.
Gedackt or Gedeckt, 65.
Gedacktbass, 68.
Gedacktflöte, 68.
Gedacktquint, 69.
Gedeckt minor, 69.
Geigenprincipal, 69.
Gemischte Stimmen, 70.
Gemshorn, 70.
Gemshornquinte, 71.
Generalcoppel, 71.
Generalcrescendo, 71.
Gleichschwebende Temperatur, 71.
Glockenspiel, 72.
Glöckleinton, 72.
Grand Bourdon, 72.
Great Quint, 72.
Gross-Cymbel, 72.
Grossgedacktbass, 73.
Grossmixtur, 73.

Harmonica, 73.
Harmonica ætherea, 74.
Harmonicabass, 74.
Harmonicaflöte, 75.
Harmonic Flute, 75.
Harmonieflöte, 75.
Harmonic Trumpet, 77.
Harmonium, 78.
Helikon, 78.

INDEX

Hellflöte, 78.
Hochdruckluft-Register, 78.
Hohlflöte, 78.
Holzflöte, 79.
Holzmaterial, 79.
Horn, 79.

Intonation, 80.

Jubalflöte, 80.

Keraulophon, 81.
Klangfarbe, 81.
Klaviertisch or Spieltischanlage, 83.
Klein-Cornett, 83.
Kleingedackt, 84.
Kleinprincipal, 84.
Kornett, 84.
Krummhorn, 84.

Labialoboe, 84.
La Force, 84.
Larigot, 84.
Lettering, 85.
Lieblich-Gedackt, 85.

Majorbass, 85.
Manual, 85.
Materials, 86.
Melodia and Double Melodia, 86.
Melodic Coupler, 86.
Melophone, 87.
Membrane, 88.
Metal, 88.
Mixture, 88.
Montre, 91.
Motor, 92.
Multiplex Registers, 92.
Musette, 92.

Nachthorn, 92.
Nasard, 93.

Nassat, 93.
Normalstimmung, 94.

Oberpedal, 94.
Obertöne, 94.
Oboe, 94.
Octave, 96.
Octave Bass, 101.
Octave Coupler, 101.
Offenflöte, 102.
Open Diapason, 102.
Ophicleide, 102.
Orchestral Clarinet, Flute, Oboe, and Violin, 103.

Pedalauslösung, 103.
Pedalcollectiven, 103.
Philomela, 104.
Physharmonica, 105.
Piccolo, 105.
Piffaro, 105.
Pneumatic Lever, 106.
Pneumatic Pistons, 108.
Portunalflöte, 110.
Posaune, 111.
Prestant, 113.
Principal, 114.
Principal Amabile, 118.
Principalbass, 118.
Principalflöte, 118.
Principal major, 118.
Probezinn, 118.
Progressio, 118.
Progressiv-Harmonica, 118.
Prolongement, 118.

Querflöte, 119.
Quintadena, 119.
Quintadena Bass, 119.
Quintatön, 119.
Quintbass, 120.
Quinte, 120.
Quintflöte, 123.

INDEX

Rauschquinte, 124.
Reed Stops, 124.
Regal, 136.
Registerausschaltungen, 137.
Registerclaviatur, 137.
Registerpneumatik, 137.
Registerwalze, 137.
Registration, 137.
Ripieno, 143.
Röhrenpneumatik, 143.
Rohrflöte, 143.
Rohrquinte, 144.
Rohrwerk, 144.
Rollschweller, 144.
Rückpositiv, 146.

Salicet, 147.
Salicional, 147.
Santflöte, 149.
Scale, 149.
Schalmei, 150.
Scharf, 151.
Schweizerflöte, 151.
Schwell-Anzeiger, 152.
Schwingungen, 152.
Septime, 152.
Seraphon, 154.
Serpent, 155.
Sesquialtera, 155.
Sifflöte, 156.
Soloclarine, 156.
Sonarpfeife, 156.
Specification, 156.
Sperrventil, 158.
Spezialcoppel, 158.
Spieltischanlagen, 158.
Spitzflöte, 158.
Spitzquinte, 159.
Spotted Metal, 159.
Stentorphon, 159.
Stentor-Sologamba, 159.
Stillgedackt, 160.
Stop-keys, 160.
Suabile, 160.

Suavial, 160.
Subbass, 160.
Suboctave Coupler, 165.
Superoctave Coupler, 165.
Swell-box, 165.
Syntematophon, 168.

Temperament, 168.
Terpodion, 169.
Tertia manu, 169.
Tertian, 170.
Tibia, 170.
Tierce, 170.
Tirasse, 171.
Tonhalle, 171.
Transmission, 173.
Tremulant, 174.
Tromba, 176.
Trombone, 176.
Trompette céleste, 176.
Trompette harmonique, 176.
Trumpet, 177.
Tuba, 180.
Tuba Mirabilis, 180.
Tubason, 182.
Tutti, 182.
Twelfth, 182.

Unda Maris, 182.
Untersatz, 183.

Vibrations, 184.
Viola, 184.
Viole d'orchestre, 186.
Violin Diapason, 186.
Violino, 186.
Violino da concerto, 186.
Violon, 187.
Violonbass, 187.
Violoncello, 187.
Voicing, 188.
Voix céleste, 189.
Volles Werk, 192.

Vox Angelica, 192.
Vox Cœlestis, 192.
Vox Humana, 193.

Waldflöte, 195.
Waldhorn, 195.
Weitpfeife, 195.

Wienerflöte, 195.
Windzeiger, 196.

Zartflöte, 197.
Zartgedackt, 197.
Zartgeige, 197.
Zinnpfeifenmaterial, 197.